Wild About Facts

For All The Things You Never Knew You Didn't Know

Wild Humphrey
The Fact Master

Elluminet Press
www.elluminetpress.com

Wild About Facts

Cover Image by Luminescent Media Ltd & Elluminet Press Ltd

Published in 2021 by Elluminet Press Ltd - www.elluminetpress.com.

Table of Contents

About the Author

Born in the United Kingdom's City of Liverpool the Author of WILD about FACTS is one of nine children and a twin. Now living on the Wirral, Wild Humphrey is married with three children and his endless Fascination with Facts has led to this book which is Fact-Packed.

'Wild Humphrey - The Fact Master' is the man with the unique ability to recall thousands of Facts and is Faster than Google. Name any day of the year and with barely a moment's thought he will tell you the significance of that day in the annals of history.

A columnist for the famous Liverpool Echo Wild Humphrey gives a fascinating and often humorous insight into what happened when and his motto seems clear when he says with a wink and a smile :

"I'll tell you all the things you never knew you didn't know".

BBC's The One Show invited Wild Humphrey into their studio to take part in a Man - v - Machine contest against Alexa, Siri and Google which he won hands-down and the 'Fact-Off' is well worth a watch. You can also catch this Fact Master on his YouTube channel.

This man with an amazing memory shares Facts about Kings, Queens, Presidents, People, Places and Iconic Events. The stories he tells are endless, inspirational, fascinating and all true and experiencing his unique delivery is like watching a Magician without the Illusion.

If you are wondering how he can do what he does he will tell you he was involved in a road accident as a child and when he left hospital and passed his exams his family joked that it must have been the bang on the head and to use his words : ***"That's a Fact"***

January

The first month of our year takes its name from Janus the Roman God of Beginnings and Endings

Janus has Two faces which look Back at the year Gone and Forward to the year Ahead

January is the Coldest month in the Northern Hemisphere and the Warmest in the Southern Hemisphere

January's Full Moon is the Wolf Moon

We are more than 50,000 kilometres Closer to the Sun in January than we are in July

There were only Ten months in our Calendar year until January and February were Added by the Romans

If you were born in January your Birthstone is Garnet

Zodiac signs for January are Capricorn and Aquarius

January 1st is New Years Day and Bloody Mary Day

January is the First of the Seven months of the Year with 31 Days giving it 744 Hours

That's a Fact !!

1st January

One of the most important Presidential orders in history was issued today in 1863 and it's powerful message would resonate across the world to this day. Abraham Lincoln issued his Emancipation Proclamation and he considered it the crowning achievement of his Presidency.

1st January

It was New Years Day 1964 when the very first ever episode of 'Top of the Pops' was shown on TV and the show quickly became a must-see. Dusty Springfield was the first singer to perform and the Beatles ended the show ***with 'I Want to Hold Your Hand' at No1.***

1st January

On New Years Day 1962 four lads from Liverpool went all the way to London to meet a music producer and were hoping for a record deal. After an hour the four hopefuls known as The Beatles were told by the boss of Decca ***they had no future in the music business.....oops!!***

1st January

The novel 'The Modern Prometheus' aka Frankenstein was published anonymously this New Year's Day in 1818 by a little known London publisher. The story was such a monster success it made this the first day of ***a very happy new year for author Mary Shelley.***

2nd January

Disaster struck at Ibrox today in 1971 after Rangers scored an injury-time equaliser against Celtic. Someone had fallen down a packed exit stairway causing a chain reaction pile-up resulting in the deaths of 66 Rangers fans ***and this tragedy took place on staircase No:13.***

2nd January

It was this January day in 1791 unsuspecting settlers in Ohio who had moved further North for a better life were attacked by angry Indians. Twelve people were killed in this bloody, unprovoked assault which is remembered to this day ***as the massacre of 'Big Bottom'.***

2nd January

It was a cold Saturday afternoon in 1982 and England were hosting Australia at Twickenham. As half-time arrived a topless young lady ran across the pitch to the roar of the crowd, her name was Erika Roe and she is ***remembered as the most famous Twickenham Streaker****.*

3rd January

This very day in 1833 Britain seized the Falkland Islands from Argentina and they have remained part of British territory ever since. Argentina tried to claim the land back by force 149 years later but their effort ***was thwarted and the Falklands remain British.***

3rd January

When Alaska was admitted to the union today in 1959 it became the 49th member of the United States and by far the largest of them all. This Final Frontier State it is larger than the 22 smallest states put together, is mostly wilderness ***and it once belonged to Russia****.*

3rd January

Earth's perihelion falls on this day each year as this is the day that we in the northern hemisphere are closer to the Sun than any other day and a full 50,000 km closer than we are in sunny July. The reason our world is so much ***colder in January is due simply to the Earth's Tilt.***

4th January

Donald Campbell was at the controls of Bluebird this afternoon in 1967 attempting a water speed record on Coniston Lake when Bluebird somersaulted through the water at high speed and Donald was killed. ***His body was finally discovered 34 years later****.*

4th January

In a barbaric act of cruelty Asian elephant 'Topsy' was executed by park officials this January afternoon 1903 in front of an invited audience at Coney Island New York. Topsy was poisoned, strangled then electrocuted ***and a movie company actually filmed her death****.*

4th January

Born today in 1809 was Frenchman Louis Braille and by the age of three an accident would cost him his eyesight. Undeterred by his misfortune Louis invented a system of raised dots known as Braille to help blind and ***partially sighted people read using their fingertips.***

5th January

Born today in 1592 was Shah Jahan, the man who created the Taj Mahal in honour of his wife who had died while giving birth to their fourteenth child. This beautiful perfectly built mausoleum is now recognised as one of ***the 'New' Seven Wonders of the World.***

5th January

Two strangers who would become notorious outlaws came face to face and what followed was a murderous crime spree where they both went along for the ride. The year was 1930 and it was this very day that ***a girl named Bonnie first met a boy named Clyde.***

5th January

It was 1066 and English King Edward the Confessor finally bowed out this very evening leaving no son and heir to the throne. This sparked a feud between three pretenders wanting the crown that would finally be settled ***nine months later at the bloody Battle of Hastings.***

5th January

Robert Louis Stevenson introduced a man with two very different personalities to the literary world today in 1886 with his must-read masterpiece that told a gothic tale of terror and it seemed avid readers everywhere ***loved to be horrified by 'Dr Jekyll and Mr Hyde'.***

6th January

King Henry VIII married his fourth wife Anne of Cleves this January afternoon in 1540 but the two had never met before and when the King first saw his new wife he was not happy. The marriage was soon annulled but Anne ***lived a good life and outlived Henry by ten years****.*

6th January

Franklyn Delano Roosevelt was America's 32nd President and he gave his famous speech of the Four Freedoms this day in 1941. Freedom of Speech, Freedom of Worship, Freedom from Want, Freedom from Harm. ***Roosevelt remains America's longest ever serving president****.*

6th January

A ferocious windstorm that struck Dublin claimed hundreds of lives and damaged thousands of properties then swept across to Liverpool where it caused more chaos and loss of life. This stormy January night in 1839 became forever known as ***'The night of the Big Wind'.***

7th January

Washington intern Monica Lewinski signed an affidavit this January day in 1998 denying her affair with Bill Clinton in the vain hope that the story would go away. Before the year was out Monica admitted the affair in detail ***and the President faced impeachment.***

7th January

Germany's Kaiser Wilhelm signed the order to bomb Britain today in 1915 during the Great War but bombers had strict instructions not to bomb the City of London in case they hit the Royal Family because the ***Royals and Kaiser Wilhelm were related to each other.***

7th January

After two years of trials, tribulations, successes and spectacular failures it was this day in 1785 that a famous journey was completed. A Frenchman and an American in a Hot Air Balloon flew from Dover to Calais to complete ***the first airborne English Channel crossing****.*

7th January

This winter's day in 1536 saw the end of the life of the very first wife of England's King Henry VIII. Katherine of Aragon had given Henry a daughter but never the son that he wanted. Henry called it quits and Katherine ***lost her King but did had manage to keep her head.***

8th January

The future King of Rock & Roll celebrated his 19th birthday today in 1954 and did so by recording his first ever two songs. Elvis sang "Casual Love" & "I'll Never Stand in Your Way" but had to pay the recording studio ***in Memphis four dollars for the privilege.***

8th January

Born today in 1935 the late, great Elvis Presley a true musical icon of the twentieth century 'The King' has topped the UK charts a record 21 times and today more people impersonate Elvis than anyone else and although ***the King has gone, his music well and truly lives on.***

8th January

The Battle of New Orleans settled the second War of Independence once and for all today in 1815. American General Andrew Jackson sent a warning to the invading British troops telling them if they dared march into Orleans ***they would be having their dinner in Hell.***

8th January

The Danes always seemed keen on England so they put an army together and invaded the country in 871 AD. But the attacking Viking force underestimated Ethelred I of Wessex and his brother Alfred the Great and were ***defeated today at the Battle of Ashdown.***

9th January

The Year was 1349, the Black Death was sweeping across Europe and in Basel Switzerland it was the Jews who got the blame. In a bid to rid the town of this terrible plague the entire Jewish population was rounded up by ***local officials and then mercilessly incinerated.***

9th January

British Prime Minister William Pitt the Younger had to find a way to pay for the Napoleonic Wars. So on this day in 1799 he introduced a temporary tax at two shillings in the pound and called it Income Tax Pitt has long since gone ***but his temporary tax still lives on****.*

9th January

When Joan of Arc went on trial today in 1431 in the French court of Reims charged with Treason her future was already doomed. This 19 year old Maid of Orleons stood accused of Heresy all because she had cut her hair short and ***dressed like a boy more than once.***

9th January

The state funeral of Horatio Nelson finally took place this Winter's day in 1806 and his body was paraded through the streets of London for all to see. Nelson's corpse had been kept in a Brandy casket for the past three months ***to keep him 'looking-good' for the big day.***

9th January

British Prime Minister William Pitt the Younger had to find a way to pay for the Napoleonic Wars. So on this day in 1799 he introduced a temporary tax at two shillings in the pound and called it Income Tax Pitt has long since gone ***but his temporary tax still lives on****.*

10th January

When the life of Coco Chanel came to and end in Paris this January afternoon in 1971 the 87 year old left an enduring legacy. The life of Coco had been colourful and controversial, her brand was a global phenomenon and ***Chanel continues to thrive, especially Chanel No5****.*

10th January

*Julius Ceasar knew that all he had to do to become leader of Rome for life was win a brutal civil war. So today in 49 BC whilst raising his sword to the heavens he defiantly shouted "****The Dye is Cast****" before he and his marching men* ***famously crossed the Rubicon.***

10th January

The London Underground opened today in 1863 It is the oldest in the world and it's 270 stations serve 11 lines. The 'Jubilee Line' opened in 1979 to commemorate the Queens Silver Jubilee. This was actually two years after ***the Queens Silver Jubilee, better late than never.***

10th January

Born today in London 1945 was a Rod Stewart and he became one of the best selling music artists of all time. 'Rod the Mod' has sold over 100 million records worldwide and even though he is now in his 70's he still sings ***'Do Ya think I'm Sexy' and the crowd still go wild.***

11th January

This January day in 1879 saw the start of the Anglo-Zulu War and British soldiers found themselves stationed in the South African Kingdom. The war lasted five months and the Battles of Isandlwana and Rorke's Drift are ***well documented in book and the film Zulu****.*

11th January

Two years before her disappearance in the Pacific Ocean and three years after her incredible flight across the Atlantic the famous American aviator Amelia Earhart flew solo today in 1935 from the beautiful Island of ***Hawaii all the way none-stop to sunny California****.*

11th January

St. Paul's Cathedral played host to the world's first national lottery draw today in 1567 after Queen Elizabeth I gave her consent. But this game was only for the rich as each entry cost Ten Shillings and the winner had to wait ***three years for their £5,000 prize.***

11th January

*Alexander Hamilton was one of the most famous men never to become American President. He was born this very morning in 1755 and became one of Americas Founding Fathers. His life ended when he lost a 'Duel' but **his face adorns the American $10 Dollar Bill**.*

12th January

*Spanish Explorer, Vasco de Balboa had discovered the Pacific Ocean and claimed it for Spain but he was hated by his jealous father-in-law and on this day in 1519 Balboa faced trumped up charges of treason. He was found **guilty, executed and his body thrown to the crows.***

12th January

An American Pima Indian who incredibly joined the Marines and fought Japanese soldiers at the Battle of Iwo Jema in WWII was born today in 1923. After the war this hero became a forgotten whisky drinking Indian until Johnny Cash recorded "The Ballad Of Ira Hayes".

12th January

*The much anticipated maiden voyage of RMS Queen Mary 2 took place today in 2004. This monumental ocean liner which is more than twice the size of the Titanic has journeyed the world, made many Atlantic crossings **and even sailed up the Mersey to Liverpool**.*

13th January

Johnny Cash was a hugely successful American singer-songwriter and one of the best selling musical artists of all time. His signature song was 'Folsom Prison Blues' and on this day in 1968 he performed a concert within the walls ***of 'Folsom Prison' and sang that very song****.*

13th January

A movie hit the big screen tonight in 1972 but due to its violent and brutal content it caused an uproar across the country. The reaction against this film was so fierce that it was later withdrawn by director Stanley Kubrick and this highly controversial film was "A Clockwork Orange".

13th January

The sinking of passenger ship Costa Concordia took place this day in 2012 with the tragic loss of 32 lives . The Captain of Concordia was later arrested on charges of manslaughter and abandoning ship, after being found guilty he ***was sentenced to 16 years imprisonment.***

14th January

Elvis Presley performed a concert this evening in Hawaii in 1973 which was watched by an estimated 1.5 billion people around the world, setting a record for a single entertainer but no one saw it in America because ***they were watching the Super Bowl instead.***

14th January

Elvis Presley performed a concert this evening in Hawaii in 1973 which was watched by an estimated 1.5 billion people around the world, setting a record for a single entertainer but no one saw it in America because ***they were watching the Super Bowl instead.***

14th January

Blonde Bombshell Marilyn Monroe tied the knot with baseball superstar Joe DiMaggio this January day in 1934 in a much publicised celebrity wedding. Then just 274 days later the marriage ended in divorce with Marilyn ***accusing her husband of mental cruelty.***

14th January

Elvis Presley was promoted to Sergeant today in 1960 whilst serving in the U.S Army and he received his three stripes. On the same day exactly thirteen years later he performed his "Aloha in Hawaii" concert to a ***worldwide audience of well over a billion people****.*

15th January

The famous event known as 'The Miracle on Hudson' took place this day in 2009 when American flight 1549 collided with Canada geese just after takeoff. Left with no choice Captain 'Sully' landed the plane in the Hudson River and ***saved the lives of all 155 people on board.***

15th January

Following her ascension to the throne two months earlier the Coronation of Queen Elizabeth I took place today in 1559 under heavy guard. The Virgin Queen soon made it clear to all would be suitors that ***she would only ever be married to her Country.***

15th January

Born this day in Atlanta Georgia 1929 was a boy who grew up to become the most famous civil rights leader the world would ever know. He was Martin Luther King Jr. and he became famous for his marches, ***his speeches and four famous words 'I have a Dream'.***

16th January

The first Emperor of Rome was appointed this January day 27 BC and his name was Augustus. During his 41 year reign the Roman Empire grew stronger than ever and Augustus proudly claimed he found Rome a city of ***stone and turned it into a city of marble.***

January 16th

Today in 1809 British General Sir John Moore, retreating to safety with his men in Spain was fatally wounded by cannon fire. His gallant action ensured his men lived to fight another day and an honorary statue of the brave ***General now stands where he fell at La Coruna.***

17th January

When Gary Gilmore was executed in Salt Lake City today in 1977 for murder it made headline news. Gilmore demanded to be executed for his crimes and his last words "Just Do It" caught the attention of sports giant ***Nike who decided to adopt them as their slogan.***

17th January

Robert Falcon Scott and his men reached the South Pole today in 1912 following a perilous journey through Antarctic sub-zero temperatures. Thinking they were the first men there, they were devastated to find ***Amundsen had reached the Pole 34 days earlier.***

18th January

When King Henry VII married Elizabeth of York today in 1486 he was determined to end to the bloody Wars of the Roses. Henry had slain his wife's uncle at Bosworth a few months earlier but Elizabeth knew her uncle was responsible ***for the disappearance of her two brothers****.*

18th January

Captain James Cook discovered a group of islands in the Pacific ocean today in 1778 and named them after the Earl of Sandwich. These Sandwich Islands were actually Hawaii and even though they now form part of the USA ***the Hawaiian flag still boasts the Union Jack****.*

18th January

A Royal Wedding took place this sunny January day in 1486 when Tudor King Henry VII took Elizabeth of York as his bride. This union brought relative calm across the country and although it seemed the Wars of the Roses ***were over there was a battle or two still to fight.***

19th January

The first Air-Raid on Britain happened today in 1915 as German Zeppelins dropped bombs killing 4 people in Norfolk. A campaign was launched saying "It is far better to face the bullets than to be killed by a bomb at home, ***Join the army at once & help to stop an air-raid"***

19th January

Thanks to the Earth's unique position in the universe the nineteenth day of this month is recognised as the coldest day of the year in the Northern Hemisphere. The good news is that everywhere will start getting warmer ***after today and Spring will soon be sprung.***

19th January

Singer Janis Joplin was born today in 1943 and amongst her songs she sings 'Oh Lord won't you buy me a Mercedes Benz'. Janis is now a member of the '27 Club' and although she never got her Mercedes Benz she was ***the proud owner of a psychedelic Porsche 356C.***

19th January

Good golly it's Dolly !! The world's most famous female Country singing superstar was born this winters day in 1946. The magnificent Dolly Parton has entertained people across the globe for years, and is well known for ***her two greatest assets - Singing and Songwriting.***

20th January

John Edgar Hoover was quite a fan of Shirley Temple and on meeting the young actress today in 1949 he gave her a rather unusual gift. After wondering what to give the girl who probably had everything the FBI boss ***presented her with a Tear Gas Fountain Pen.***

20th January

America's 40th President was Ronald Reagan and he finally left office today in 1989 after serving two presidential terms. On doing so Reagan became the country's first President in 149 years to have been voted ***into office in a '0' year and actually come out alive.***

20th January

The first three Astronauts to reach the moon were born in 1930 and the first was born today. His name is Buzz Aldrin and 'Buzz' became so popular they named a toy after him and that toy has ***spent longer in outer-space than Buzz Aldrin did himself.***

20th January

The reign of George V came to an end today in 1936 when he died with his doctor by his side. This King had led the country through WWI, changed the Royal name to Windsor and made the first Royal Christmas Broadcast ***but his last words were "Bugger Bognor".***

21st January

French King Louis XVI was marched through the Parisian streets this day in Paris 1793 for execution during the French Revolution. The guillotine's 'blade of death' awaited the King and in France this heavily used form of ***execution was preferred to the bloody Axe.***

21st January

*When Russian Grigori Rasputin was born today in 1869 nobody knew the colourful life he would lead. Rasputin was the Mystic they called the 'Mad Monk' who's midnight murder would one day inspire Boney-M to sing "****Ra Ra Rasputin Lover of the Russian Queen.....".***

21st January

When Concorde flew its first commercial flight today in 1976 two flights took to the skies, flying London to Bahrain and Paris to Rio de Janeiro. Cheers rang out and champagne flowed then for another twenty seven years ***the supersonic Concorde graced the skies.***

22nd January

Apple took centre stage during half time at Super Bowl XVIII today to advertise their home computer and in a parody of George Orwell's '1984' the advert showed a running girl smashing a hammer into a giant screen with ***Big Brother announcing "1984 won't be like 1984"***

22nd January

In 1908 USA a lady named Katie was arrested and hauled before a Judge today for lighting a cigarette in public. Katie defiantly told the Judge "I have just as much right to smoke as you have. No man shall dictate to me."- ***Now that was a good bit of Girl Power.***

22nd January

The late, great Dixie Dean born today in 1907 became Everton's greatest ever goalscorer. After joining the Blues from Tranmere, Dixie became one of the true all time Goodison greats, scoring an incredible ***SIXTY League goals in the 1927/28 season alone.***

22nd January

The year was 1901 and the long reign of Queen Victoria ended this very day meaning Edward VII could finally ascend to the throne. He had waited longer than anybody else to wear the crown and as King he promoted ***tweed outfits, cigars and a traditional Sunday roast.***

23rd January

The Earl of Moray was the first head of government killed with a firearm when he was assassinated today in 1570. Some believed that "They killed the Earl of Moray and Lady Mondegreen" but actually 'They Killed the ***Earl of Moray and laid him on the green'****.*

23rd January

The first induction to the Rock 'N' Roll Hall of Fame took place today in 1986 and among the inductees were Chuck Berry, James Brown, Ray Charles, Fats Domino, J.L. Lewis, The Everly Brothers, Buddy Holly and of course the ***King of Rock 'N' Roll himself Elvis Presley.***

23rd January

Over 3,000 Zulu warriors attacked 150 British Troops stationed at Rorkes Drift today in 1879 but the highly disciplined soldiers fought an almighty battle forcing the Zulus to retreat. The incredible battle has since been ***immortalised in the must-watch movie Zulu****.*

23rd January

It was during the Second Boer War in South Africa this day in 1900 the lives of almost 250 British troops were lost in battle. The men had been stranded on a hill of stone in dense fog with the enemy above and below ***and were killed at the Battle of 'Spion Kop'.***

24th January

Claudius became leader of Rome today in 41AD following the brutal assassination of his nephew Caligula. The new Emperor was slightly deaf and walked with a limp so his enemies left him alone and he reigned for ***13 years before being poisoned by his wife.***

24th January

When the life of wartime prime minister Winston Churchill ended today in 1965 he was 90 years old and fully deserved his state funeral some days later. In a twist of fate his father Randolph Churchill also died this ***very same day exactly seventy years earlier.***

24th January

Roman Emperor Caligula was assassinated by his own guards this January night 41 AD after just four years in power. Caligula's rule was evil and cruel, his terror had taken its toll on the people of Rome so he was brutally ***murdered and replaced by his uncle Claudius****.*

25th January

Burns Night is celebrated around the globe this night every year in memory of Scottish poet Robert Burns who was born this January day 1759. For a man who lived for just 37 years 'Rabbie' left quite a legacy including ***the words for the tune of 'Auld Lang Syne'.***

25th January

It was 1995 and that team at the other end of the M62 were playing Crystal Palace when their talisman was sent off by the referee. This was the night Eric Cantona jumped into the crowd to Kung-Fu kick a fan on the terraces after ***the red mist descended on the Frenchman****.*

25th January

Edward III ascended to the English throne today in 1327 following the forced abdication of his father some months earlier. This fearless new leader later banished his mother to the coast, had her lover executed ***and then started the Hundred Years War with France****.*

25th January

Notorious Chicago gangster Al Capone breathed his last this January night in 1947 and went to meet his maker. Capone orchestrated the St Valentine's Day massacre, amassed a fortune during prohibition years and his business ***card read 'second hand furniture dealer'.***

25th January

King Henry VIII married his already pregnant second wife, Anne Boleyn today in a 1533 secret ceremony. Those present were sworn to absolute silence and spoke not a word but the marriage ended badly for Anne as ***she was beheaded for Treason three years later****.*

January 26th

The largest diamond in the world discovered today 1905 in South Africa was named after the mine in which it was found. The 3,000 carat Cullinan diamond was broken up and presented to King Edward VII for his 66th birthday ***and now forms part of the Crown Jewels.***

26th January

Today is Australia Day which celebrates the arrival of the British First Fleet in 1788 when the ships that had left the shores of England eight months earlier finally sailed into what is now Sydney Harbour. There will be plenty of partying ***as there is each year this day down under****.*

26th January

*Following several successful tests John Logie Baird gave his first public demonstration of a working television set to a group of people today in London 1926. The picture was black & white and a jubilant Baird declared "****One day people just might own their own TV set****".*

27th January

Edward John Smith was born this very day in 1850 in Staffordshire and sixty two years later it was he who Captained of the world's most famous ship 'The Titanic' Edward had lived for a while with his wife in the Waterloo, ***Liverpool and his daughter was born there.***

27th January

A baby born this January day in Austria 1756 grew up to be a musical genius and his name was Wolfgang Amadeus Mozart. Although this maestro would only live to the age of 35 his everlasting legacy has influenced many ***future classical composers including Beethoven****.*

27th January

German death camp Auschwitz was finally liberated this January day in 1945 by Russian troops who smashed their way in and overpowered the Nazis. Five years of horror at Auschwitz were finally at an end but ***tragically the liberation was too late for so many.***

28th January

A day shared by two Tudor Kings for very different reasons. Henry VII the victor at Bosworth field who brought the Tudor dynasty to the throne was born today in Monmouth in 1457 and his son Henry VIII the most ***notorious King of them all, died today in 1547****.*

28th January

Disaster struck today in 1986 as people watched NASA spaceship Challenger explode before their very eyes seconds after take-off. All 7 onboard this terror trip perished including civilian Christa McCauliffe who joined the crew to be ***the first ever school teacher in Space.***

29th January

The Victoria Cross was established today in 1856 as the highest award in the UK Honours system. Queen Victoria wanted to properly recognise gallantry in the presence of the enemy to members of the British ***armed forces particularly in the Crimean war****.*

29th January

When King George III went to meet his maker today in 1820 he was and still is the country's longest reigning King ever to wear the British Crown. George was from the House of Hanover and during his turbulent reign ***things went from Good to Bad to Ugly.***

29th January

Less than a year after India gained independence from Britain their bespectacled leader Gandhi was assassinated today in 1848. The man who despised the British and campaigned tirelessly for independence was ***gunned down by one of his own countrymen****.*

30th January

Franklyn Delano Roosevelt was born today in New York 1882 but he wasn't the healthiest child in the world and after having developed Polio could barely walk. But this didn't stop him becoming the 32nd President of America ***and the longest serving President of them all.***

30th January

King Charles I was kneeling on the scaffold this winter's morning in 1649 waiting for the axeman to strike when he heard the blade scrape. The King turned to his executioner saying "Hurt not the thing that is going to hurt your king" ***moments later his head was off.***

30th January

This afternoon in 1969 the world's most famous band gave their final ever concert. An impromptu performance from the Beatles on a rooftop above Savile Row lasting 42 minutes the final song they sang was Get Back and ***the Fab Four never performed together again****.*

31st January

Guy Fawkes had been caught red handed with thirty six barrels of gunpowder attempting to blow up the Houses of Parliament and today in 1606 he and his accomplices having been found guilty of High Treason were ***hanged, drawn and quartered in Westminster****.*

31st January

There was chaos in Moscow this January day in 1990 as almost 30,000 people made their way to the town centre to enjoy something new. The commotion was caused by the opening of Russia's first McDonalds restaurant ***and everyone it seemed, wanted a Big Mac.***

31st January

Ex-Beatle George Harrison enjoyed the sweet taste of solo success today in 1971 as his beautifully sung song 'My Sweet Lord' was on top of the UK charts. The quiet Beatle had become the first of the Fab-Four to have ***a solo No:1 song since the break-up of the band****.*

February

Taking it's name from the Latin Februum meaning Purification - This Is the Month of Love & Romance

February has 28 days in a Common Year and 29 each Leap Year making it 'The Only Month that Grows'

The Welsh sometimes refer to February as "y mis Bach" which translates as the "Little Month"

February in the Northern Hemisphere is equivalent to August in the Southern Hemisphere

February and January were added by The Romans to extend our Calendar from 10 to 12 Months

The Snow Moon belongs to February and is the Only Moon not Guaranteed to appear Every Year

To Be February Born makes Amethyst your Birthstone with Aquarius & Pisces your Zodiac Signs

The name February is one of the most mis-pronounced and mis-spelt words in the English Language

That's a Fact !!

February 1st

This is the first day of the shortest month of the year as February only has 672 hours which are boosted to 696 each Leap Year. The God of February and is associated with death and purification but this month is all ***about Love & Romance so enjoy the next 28 days****.*

1st February

What am I going to do about Mary? This was a question only Queen Elizabeth I could answer and this Queen of England finally conquered that Royal conundrum today in 1587 when she signed the death warrant for ***the cousin she had never met - Mary Queen of Scots.***

2nd February

Nell Gwynn was born on this day in 1650 and became the mistress of King Charles II although she called him her Charles the 1st. On his deathbed the King famously said "Let not poor Nelly starve" after which Nell received ***a handsome yearly payment from the Crown.***

2nd February

One of the world's greatest literary works of art was published this day in 1922 The masterpiece entitled 'Ulysses' written by James Joyce tells a delightful tale of two days in Dublin and introduces the reader to many things ***including the wonderful palindrome – Tattarrattat.***

3rd February

Woodrow Wilson was the 28th American President and he wasn't particularly fond of Britain he served two terms as president, guided America through WWI and married whilst in office. He was never a man of good health and ***he finally bowed out on this day in 1924.***

3rd February

It was today in Brooklyn 1971 a Police officer was shot in the face during a drugs bust after corrupt fellow officers ignored his calls for assistance. Hollywood just had to make a movie to tell us the tale and it was ***Al Pacino who played the Police Officer they called - Serpico.***

4th February

Facebook was founded today in 2004 by Mark Zuckerberg and friends in Harvard. This phenomenon leads the social media world and is now so vast that if Facebook were a country it would be the third largest in the world ***by population behind China and India****.*

4th February

After being kidnapped and held for ransom in Austria for 14 months Richard the Lionheart was finally released today in 1194. The English had patriotically raised the money to buy the King his freedom and ***the 100,000 they paid was most certainly a King's Ransom.***

4th February

It was this February day in 1912 that high flying Franz Reichelt jumped from the Eiffel Tower in his ready-to-wear parachute suit. People watched and cheered as the Frenchman courageously leapt from the top of the Tower ***but moments later - SPLAT !!***

5th February

Apollo 14 touched down on the surface of the Moon today in 1971 ten months after its predecessor had failed. One of the Astronauts on board was Alan Shepard who enjoyed his own claim to fame as the first American in space ***and also the oldest man on the Moon.***

5th February

On a very muddy pitch this afternoon in 1972 Ronnie Radford scored one of the greatest FA Cup goals ever. He hit a thunderous strike to help lowly Hereford United beat the might of Newcastle and the young match ***commentator that day was a certain John Motson.***

5th February

In 1597 a newly appointed Japanese government didn't take kindly to people preaching Christianity as it 'posed a threat to society'. So a group of early Japanese Christians known as the 26 Martyrs of Japan were ***arrested today then taken to Nagasaki and crucified.***

5th February

*Laker Airways collapsed this February day in 1982 and resulted in many job losses for the North West. For over fifteen years Sir Freddie Laker had taken on aviation's big boys and the end of his company meant you could no longer "***Fly with Freddie" or "Take a Laker"***.*

6th February

James II ascended to the English throne today in 1685 and 'Dismal Jimmy' as he was known made the huge mistake of trying to revert the country to Catholicism. Within four years the new King faced the Glorious Revolution, ***abdicated his throne then fled to France.***

February 6th

Queen Elizabeth II ascended to the throne today in 1952 whilst in a tree house during a visit to Kenya. Elizabeth left England as princess then returned as Queen and is Britain's longest reigning monarch and like her ***namesake before her Elizabeth was 25 upon ascension****.*

6th February

When the Representation of the People Act was passed by Parliament today in 1918 women in Great Britain finally had the right to vote. It was a bit half-hearted though as the female voter had to meet ***minimum property qualifications and be over 30 years of age.***

6th February

This day in 1685 was the end of the line for the longest reigning Stuart King Charles II as he succumbed to illness and went to meet his maker. Unfortunately Charles left no son and heir to the throne so the Crown passed ***to his younger brother 'Dismal Jimmy'.***

7th February

The majestic supersonic aircraft Concorde flew its fastest ever flight from New York to London today in 1996 crossing the pond and touching down in just 2Hours 59minutes 54seconds. This was the only aircraft in which people could ***fly Supersonic and drink Gin & Tonic.***

7th February

The first investiture of an English Prince of Wales took place at Caernarfon Castle today in 1301 and the man bestowed was Edward of Caernarfon. His father King Edward I had built the great castle in the late 13th century and ***his son and heir had also been born there****.*

7th February

A 2,000 year old Roman vase on display at the British Museum had pride of place in a glass case until today in 1845 when a drunken man visiting the museum smashed the priceless Vase to pieces. The man was arrested and prosecuted ***but fined just £3.00 for his crime.***

8th February

*When the life of Sir Giles Gilbert Scott ended this evening in 1960 he left an enduring legacy. This man designed the world famous Red Telephone Box and Liverpool's very own Anglican Cathedral and **inside the Cathedral there now stands a Red Telephone Box. Hello?***

8th February

*This was 1983 and one of the most famous Epsom Derby winners of all time vanished into the night after being stolen from his stud farm in Ireland. The horse was Shergar and despite investigations into his disappearance **neither the horse nor the thieves were ever found.***

February 8th

*This afternoon in 1587 Mary Queen of Scots was beheaded on the orders of Elizabeth I at Fotheringhay Castle Northamptonshire and to the disbelief of those watching the Bloody execution a very nervous axeman **took several attempts to chop off the Queen's head.***

8th February

*Groundbreaking for the Hollywood 'Walk of Fame' started today in 1960 so people could be recognised for great personal achievement with their very own Star on the famous Boulevard. Lots of people have a Star these days **and there's even one for Donald Trump.***

9th February

*The world witnessed three major aviation achievements in 1969. There was the Moon landing in July, the flight of Concorde in March and today was the first ever flight of the Boeing 747 Jumbo Jet which helped coin the famous phrase "**If it ain't Boeing, I ain't going**".*

9th February

*A girl named Lydia Pinkham born today in 1819 became popular in Victorian England due to her home made potions and lotions. Lydia seemed to have a medicinal compound for every ailment and thanks to a novelty No:1 song by the Scaffold **we know her as 'Lily The Pink'.***

9th February

*In 1960's America the place to be on TV was The Ed Sullivan show and this evening in 1964 The Beatles made their debut. Beatlemania had gone Boom in the USA and thanks to the Fab Four an audience of over **73 million Americans tuned in to watch the show**.*

9th February

*After many years in the making the Boeing 747 'Jumbo Jet' took to the skies today in 1969 making its first test flight. It was Pan-Am who became the first airline to operate the mighty 747 and although Pan-Am are long since gone **the gigantic Jumbo flies on and on and on.***

10th February

The lifeless body of Lord Darnley was found in the early hours of this cold February morning in 1567 and it was soon established he had been strangled. Rumours quickly spread as to whom the culprits were and fingers were pointing ***directly at his wife Mary Queen of Scots.***

10th February

Glen Miller and his orchestra became the first music artists to be awarded Gold for sales topping the 1 Million mark and today in 1942 they received their coveted Disc. The crazy little melody that earned them this distinction ***was entitled "Chattanooga Choo Choo".***

10th February

Chess grandmaster Garry Kasparov competed in a six-game chess match against IBM computer 'Deep Blue' today in 1996 under tournament conditions. Victory by 4–2 went to Kasparov and the chess genius ***was ranked World No1 until retirement 19 years later****.*

10th February

A Royal Wedding took place this February day in 1840 when British Queen Victoria married Prince Albert of Germany and cheers rang out across the country. Queen proposed to her Prince some months earlier ***and during their 21 year marriage they had 9 children.***

11th February

Born today in 1969 Los Angeles was the fabulous Jennifer Aniston who achieved greatness as one of the six Friends in the still incredibly popular TV show of the same name. Since the show finished Jennifer has gone on ***to be by far the most successful of all 6 Friends.***

11th February

Scotland hosted South Africa in a rugby match in 1970 and 96 people were arrested and fined a total of £1,344 for protesting against the visiting team. Then a man stepped forward today and kindly paid all fines in full for everyone ***and this man's name was John Lennon.***

11th February

Millions of fans were shocked when the life of multi-talented singing superstar Whitney Houston came to a tragic end today in 2012. Whitney was staying at the Beverley Hills Hilton Hotel where she was found after ***drowning in a bath of boiling water in room No: 434.***

11th February

Many in the world of boxing were shocked this 1990 night but none more than Mike Tyson. It was fight night in Tokyo when relatively unknown Buster Douglas sent Tyson crashing to the canvas and for the first time in his career ***Iron Mike was counted out on the canvas.***

12th February

A murder that shocked a nation took place this February afternoon in 1993 when 2 year old James Bulger was abducted from a busy shopping centre in Liverpool. The shocking series of events that led to the little boy's death ***were carried out by two other children.***

12th February

Abraham Lincoln was born this February day in 1809 and grew up to become the 16th and most famous American President. Lincoln was the first Republican ever to hold office and the first thing he had to do was guide the country ***through a very bloody American Civil War.***

12th February

The Rat, The Ox, The Tiger, The Rabbit, The Dragon, The Snake, The Horse, The Ram, The Monkey, The Rooster, The Dog, The Pig are the 12 signs of the Chinese Zodiac. As Chinese communities celebrate New Year today they'll ***say goodbye to the Rat and Hello to the Ox.***

12th February

Teenage Protestant Lady Jane Grey was taken to the gallows today in 1554 and beheaded on the orders of the English Catholic Queen Mary I. These two Tudors would be remembered for very different reasons ***one as the Nine Day Queen and the other as Bloody Mary.***

13th February

It was the early hours of this morning in 1692 the shocking 'Massacre of Glencoe' took place. The McDonalds had helped the Campbells, giving them food, water and friendship then in the dark of night the Campbells ***turned on their sleeping hosts and murdered them.***

13th February

The famous 16th Century Italian Astronomer Galileo Galilei was in Rome today in 1633 after being summoned to face trial by Inquisition Galileo had found himself in hot water and was forced to withdraw his outrageous suggestion ***that the Earth revolved around the Sun.***

13th February

It was unlucky 13 for the young Catherine Howard, *fifth wife of Henry VIII, as queen she had committed adultery against her King and was guilty of Treason. Catherine was executed this cold winter's morning in 1542,* ***her slender neck no match for the Axeman's blade.***

13th February

The quiet city of Dresden was so beautiful and its architecture so compelling it could easily rival the likes of Florence and Venice. Then this February night in 1945 Bomber Harris laid siege to the city and British bombs ***rained down on Dresden and destroyed it.***

14th February

St Valentine of Rome** was locked up for disobeying the Emperor's orders and whilst imprisoned he fell in love with his jailers daughter. When leaving his cell to face execution this day in 269 AD he handed a loving note **to his sweetheart signed................'Your Valentine'.

14th February

*King Richard II breathed his last today in the year 1400 just five months after his forced abdication. Henry IV had usurped the throne from the young King and kept him locked up in Pontefract Castle then to get rid of Richard permanently **Henry starved him to death**.*

14th February

*This should have been a lovely romantic Valentine's evening in 2013 for Reeva Steenkamp but it turned into terror as she was shot and killed by Oscar Pistorius in his apartment. A media circus surrounded the trial that followed before **the killer was eventually put in prison.***

14th February

*In a ceremonial act soldiers laid down their arms this Valentine's Day in 1660 then immediately picked them up again. They then swore allegiance to King Charles II and from that day to this Cromwell's New Model Army have **been known as the Coldstream Guards**.*

15th February

Seventeenth Century Mathematician Isaac Newton was also one of the most influential scientists of all time and was always looking to the future. Then in a note he wrote today in 1676 Newton declared: "If I have seen further, ***it is by Standing on the Shoulders of Giants".***

15th February

When American battleship Maine was sunk in a Cuban harbour this afternoon in 1898 the U.S. immediately blamed Spain and declared war. Victory for America quickly followed but further investigations found the sinking of Maine ***had absolutely nothing to do with Spain.***

15th February

Today marks the 50th Anniversary *of Decimalisation in Britain as Pounds, Shillings and Pence were replaced by the all new 'Decimal Currency' there had been a five year countdown to this D-Day but as the day unfolded* ***not everything went quite to plan – Oops !!***

15th February

Chaos reigned supreme across much of the country this February day in 1971 as we moved away from Pounds Shillings and Pence and Decimal Currency took centre stage. It was a case of out with the old and in with the new as ***the UK had officially been Decimalised.***

16th February

Unveiled to the world this day in 1998 *was Andrew Gormley's 'Angel of the North' statue standing 66ft tall in Gateshead. The wings of the Angel are designed so that if you were tall enough she could give you a hug and* ***if you ever travel along the A1 she's unmissable.***

16th February

A painted sign displayed in the centre of Munich today in 1943 which read "Out with Hitler! Long live freedom" had been left by the none violent university student group known as 'White Rose'. But sadly within just a few days ***the students were all arrested and beheaded****.*

16th February

When Howard Carter opened Tutankhamen's Tomb today in 1923 he was disturbing an Egyptian King laid to rest 4,000 years earlier. The events that followed led superstitious locals to announce the opening of this Tomb ***had unleashed the Deadly Curse of the Pharaohs.***

17th February

Born today in 1940 Connecticut was the American singer songwriter and sixties heartthrob Gene Pitney. Gene had a gallery of hits to his name and travelled the globe singing his songs but it always seemed no matter where he went ***he was only 24 hours from Tulsa.***

17th February

The second son of Henry VII & Elizabeth of York attended Caernarfon Castle this February day in 1502 for his investiture as the new Prince of Wales. But this Prince had eyes on a much bigger prize and perhaps thought - ***Why be a Prince when I can be a notorious King.***

17th February

Mount Everest is the world's highest mountain *and man first reached its summit in 1953. Then more climbers managed to reach the top every Summer for next twenty seven years but it was this day in 1980 that* ***this great Mountain was first climbed in the Winter.***

18th February

Born today in 1954 was John Travolta who became a famous singer dancer and actor starring in Grease, Saturday Night Fever and more. Things went quiet for the superstar until Quentin Tarantino needed a Pulp Fiction hitman and said to Travolta ***"You're the one that I want"***

18th February

A small planet, over 4.6 Billion miles from Earth *discovered today in 1930 was later named after the God of the underworld 'Pluto'. Then in 2006 the planet was reclassified as a 'Dwarf Planet' and since it's discovery* ***'Pluto' has still not completed an orbit around the Sun.***

18th February

*The second American War of Independence AKA the War of 1812 came to an end this February day in 1815 after President James Madison signed the Treaty of Ghent. The Americans had ended this rather pointless war **but then again, they had started it.***

18th February

*The Wars of the Roses were in full throttle and Edward IV was King of the country but he had a brother George who was Duke of Clarence. The King suspected George was up to no good and had him executed today in 1478 privately and **quietly inside The Tower of London.***

19th February

*Parents of a four year old girl in Idaho wanted to send their daughter to her grandparents 73 miles away so they put her in a mail bag today in 1914 and sent her by post. As the child weighed under 50 lbs this option **cost much less than paying for a train ticket.***

19th February

*Nine years ago today a brutal fight broke out at the notorious Apodaca prison in Mexico as tensions reached boiling point between rival in-mates. Hardened prisoners who hated each other were out for blood and **by the time the brawl was over 44 of them were dead.***

19th February

Aaron Burr is the American** Vice President who fought a 'Pistols at Dawn' duel and emerged the victor but on this day in 1807 he was arrested on charges of Treason and thrown in jail. People forgot all about Burr but the man he killed **adorns the back of the U.S. $10 Bill.

20th February

*The most famous Ballet in the world received it's much anticipated premier this February evening in Moscow 1877 and is a masterpiece by Composer Tchaikovsky. A Princess named Odette is turned into a swan by an evil sorcerer **in this compelling story of Swan Lake.***

20th February

*The USA finally made things even in the space-race today in 1962 when space-ship 'Friendship 7' took off from Florida with Astronaut John Glenn at the controls. Glenn became the first American to orbit the Earth and **could definitely say he had flown far far away.***

20th February

*When the son of Henry VIII and Jayne Seymour was crowned Edward VI of England today in 1547 he was just nine years old and the first Protestant to ascend to the throne. Poor health meant the young King would reign just six years **and when he died all hell broke loose.***

20th February

The English FA Premiere League was founded today in 1992 and within months of it's formation all 22 clubs in the old 1st Division left the Football League to embrace the riches of the all new Premiership which is now ***the most watched sports league in the world.***

21st February

The town of Arles in France is well known as the dwelling for Vincent Van Gogh but on this day in 1875 a baby girl named Jeanne Calment was born there and Jeanne became the oldest living person on record living to ***the age of 122 yrs and 164 days in that same French town.***

21st February

The Nazis started building their barbaric death camp Austwich today in 1940 and within a few months thousands of unsuspecting people were taken in and what followed was horrific. The words above the entrance to this place of death ***translate as - Work sets you free.***

21st February

Malcolm X was assassinated by three members of the Nation of Islam today in 1965 the group from which he had split just weeks earlier. His influence in the group was so strong that membership numbers grew from 1,000 to 40,000 ***but some just didn't like it when he left.***

21st February

They had been around for some time and many people felt trapped by them but then on this February day 1952 the unexpected actually happened. Winston Churchill's Government scrapped National Identity Cards and declared ***it was time to 'Set the people free'.***

22nd February

A boy named Robert Wadlow born today in 1918 in the American State of Illinois became the world's tallest man after growing over 8 feet 11 inches tall. This Gentle Giant as he was known died at the age of just twenty-two ***following a cut he received to his ankle****.*

22nd February

It was in New York that Frank Winfield Woolworth opened his very first store today in 1878 and it marked the beginning of a meteoric rise for his company. This was the place where everything cost five cents and ***people were soon talking about the Wonder of Woollies.***

22nd February

America had waited eight years for an Olympic payback against Russia and today in 1980 they finally got their wish. Against all the odds the Americans managed to beat an all-star Russian Ice Hockey Marvels in what ***became known as the 'Miracle on Ice'.***

22nd February

A man threw a grenade into the U.S. Embassy in Montenegro this February afternoon in 2018 but nothing happened and no-one was hurt. Moments later a second explosion went off and he got more than he bargained for ***because he was the one who was killed.***

23rd February

A bloody conflict in American history started this February day 1836 and this was a pivotal event in the Texas Revolution. William Travis, Jim Bowie, Davy Crockett and another 200 brave men fought to the death against ***1,800 Mexican soldiers at the Battle of the Alamo.***

23rd February

One of the world's most iconic photographs was taken this February day in 1945 during WWII after US troops had successfully invaded the Japanese island. The incredible image shows six US Marines raising Old Glory during ***the fierce bloody battle of Iwo Jima.***

23rd February

The Battle of the Alamo today in 1836 "180 were challenged by Travis to die, by the line that he drew with his sword when the battle was nigh, any man that would fight to the death cross over but him that would live better fly, ***and over the line went 179" Johnny Cash.***

23rd February

Following the Glorious Revolution of 1688 England needed a new King and William of Orange was proclaimed just that man today in 1689. But new rules applied to the monarchy which meant that like it or not ***William III would have to rule jointly with his wife Mary.***

24th February

The last invasion of Britain ended today in 1797 after just two days when 1,400 French soldiers surrendered at Fishguard. They thought they were facing Elite Guards of England but it turns out they laid down their arms ***to an army of local Welsh women in tall black hats.***

24th February

Andrew Johnson the 17th American President lost an impeachment vote today in 1868 and was the first of two Presidents ever impeached, the second being Bill Clinton. Both held onto office, one by the skin of his teeth, ***the other by the elastic in his underpants.***

24th February

Prince Charles announced his engagement to 19 year old Lady Diana Spencer this February afternoon in 1981 and 4 months later Charles and his blushing Bride tied the knot. But the relationship was doomed from the start and ***it didn't end well - particularly for Diana.***

24th February

Johnny Cash The Man in Black performed a concert this afternoon in 1969 at San Quentin Penitentiary. To the delight of the prisoners he sang about the destruction of San Quentin itself and for the very first time sang A boy named Sue ***and even the guards seemed to enjoy it.***

25th February

French artist Renoir was born today in 1841 and became a leader in Impressionist painting. He was well known for works of art showing feminine sensuality and painted 1,000's of female images then in his later years arthritis meant ***brushes had to be bound to his hands.***

25th February

When Sir Christopher Wren passed away peacefully today in 1723 at the grand age of 90 he certainly left an enduring legacy. During his lifetime the multi-talented Wren was one of the world's most highly acclaimed Architects and ***his masterpiece is St Paul's Cathedral.***

25th February

World heavyweight champion Sonny Liston faced a young boxer from Louisville tonight in 1965 he was odds on favourite to keep his crown. The bell rang for Round 7 but Liston refused to fight any further and the stunned boxing world ***had a new champion named Cassius Clay.***

26th February

The trial of an Austrian man charged with Treason for his part in the infamous 'Beer Hall Putsch' began today in Munich 1924 and he was soon found guilty. Although he was locked up perhaps they should have thrown away ***the key because this criminal was Adolf Hitler.***

26th February

One of the most famous and most watched events in the horse racing calendar is the Grand National steeplechase and the first ever official Aintree Grand National race took place this February afternoon in 1839 when ***17 horses ran and the lucky winner was Lottery.***

27th February

The twelfth Aintree Grand National took place today in 1850 and the winning horse was named Abd-Al-Kader. This galloping Irish outsider crossed the finish line to become the first dual winner of this famous steeplechase and ***the first horse ever to win in consecutive years.***

28th February

An anti-government uprising in Taiwan ended very badly for those involved today in 1947 as troops moved in to quell the unrest. This protest was put down so violently it resulted in the deaths of almost 28,000 people and ***is remembered as the February 28th Massacre.***

29th February

The Earth take 365 days to complete its orbit around the Sun plus a few hours more. For this cosmic reason we gain an additional day every four years to give us the 29th day of February and if you were born this day it makes you ***a Leap-ling which ain't such a bad thing.***

29th February

Dating back to fifth century Ireland women were given this one day every 4 years to propose if their man was taking too long and if he didn't accept there was a forfeit to pay. Women can propose when they to want these days ***which kind of takes away the mystique.***

29th February

When Leap-day falls every four years Leap-lings can celebrate their birthday properly but for the other 3 this birthday is legally declared as 'the day after the 28th February'. If this is the day you were born you are not alone - ***5 million people are born this day every 4 years.***

March

March is From Martius and is Named after the All Conquering Roman God of War - The Mighty Thor

March was once The First Month of our Calendar Year until The Romans Added Two more

The Spring Equinox in the Northern Hemisphere takes place in March after which the Hours of Daylight Hours last Longer

Because The Clocks Spring Forward in March This 31 Day Month has 743 Hours instead of 744

March Heralds the Beginning of Spring in the Northern Hemisphere and Autumn in the Southern Hemisphere

The Birthstone for March is the Aquamarine and the Zodiac signs for this Month are Pisces & Aries

Celebrations take place for Two Saints this month - March 1st St. David's Day and March 17th St. Patrick's Day

For the Romans it was Martius that Heralded the Start of the Season of Warfare

That's a Fact !!

1st March

Aviator Charles Lindbergh went to his son's bedroom this evening in 1932 only to find a $50,000 ransom note waiting for him. Charles Jnr had been taken and tragically for the Lindberghs the kidnapping very quickly ***led to the terrible death of their 20 month old baby boy.***

1st March

It was this day in 1872 over 2 million acres of land in the U.S. known as Yellowstone was officially dedicated by President Ulysses S. Grant as the world's first National Park. This amazing piece of planet Earth sits atop a volcano ***and is home to the famous geyser - Old Faithful.***

2nd March

King Kong was shown in cinemas for the first time this March evening in 1933 and cinema goers were in awe as they saw Kong climb atop the Empire State Building only to be shot down but everybody knows the planes ***didn't get him - It was Beauty who killed the Beast****.*

2nd March

*A movie premier this March evening in 1965 introduced audiences to the singing and dancing Von Trapp family and starred Julie Andrews alongside Christopher Plummer. Anyone who has ever seen this film knows all too well "****The Hills are Alive with the Sound of Music****".*

3rd March

*Carmen is one of the most popular operas in the world today but when this story first took to a Parisian stage tonight in 1875 there was stunned silence. The play was later described as so vulgar that audiences **had been scandalised by obscenity and immorality**.*

3rd March

*It was today in Edinburgh in 1847 Alexander Graham Bell was born and he is the man credited with the invention of the Telephone. Alexander phoned lots of people to chit chat but never did he ever phone his mother or **his wife Mabel - As both of them were deaf.***

4th March

*The notorious Kray twins were sentenced to Life imprisonment today in 1969 after being found Guilty of murder and their stranglehold on London's gangland was over. Ronnie and Reggie would never again walk **the streets of London and both men would die behind bars.***

4th March

*Many fans of Liverpool Football Club will know Kenny Dalglish was born this very day in 1951 and without doubt he became one of the club's greatest players as well as remarkable manager. A true ambassador on **and off the pitch - Happy birthday King Kenny**.*

5th March

One of Russia's most brutal dictators died this March afternoon in 1953 and his name was Joseph Stalin. For thirty years he ruled the largest country in the world with an iron fist and during that time was ***responsible for the deaths of millions of his countrymen.***

5th March

The first of England's Plantagenet Kings was born this warm March day in 1133 in Le Mans France and at the age of 21 was crowned King Henry II. His wife was Eleanor of Aquitaine and they were the parents of ***Richard the Lionheart and the King named John.***

5th March

British soldiers on duty in Boston Massachusetts today in 1770 didn't mind too much when a crowd of Americans threw snowballs at them. But when snowballs turned to sticks and stones the soldiers picked up their rifles ***aimed at the crowd and shot five of them dead***

6th March

When news of the death of Victoria the last Hawaiian Princess broke today in 1899 her people were devastated. Victoria had been on a doomed crusade to save her country from the clutches of America and it was declared ***the young Princess died from a broken heart****.*

6th March

A different kind of food went on sale for the first time today in 1930 across stores in Springfield Massachusetts. No one had seen frozen food before but its popularity was such that it soon became a global phenomenon and ***the man responsible was Clarence Birdseye.***

6th March

The recently crowned world heavyweight boxing champion Cassius Clay got the name change he wanted when he met with Nation of Islam leader Elija Muhammad. It was 1964 and this was the day the boxer became ***Muhammad Ali and was never again called Clay.***

7th March

Some say nothing can change the shape of things to come and those words were perhaps never more true than today in 1936 as Germany reoccupied the Rhineland. This act was in complete violation of the Treaty of Versailles ***which the Germans had signed 17 years earlier.***

7th March

Divers found the crew cabin of Space Shuttle Challenger on the Ocean floor today in 1986 with the bodies of all crew members still inside. NASA has never exactly concluded their actual cause of death but the final moments for these ***seven Astronauts must have been terrifying.***

7th March

Henry VIII had his divorce request rejected by the Pope this day in 1530 and was none too pleased. Determined to divorce Catherine of Aragon the resourceful King ignored the Pope broke from the Catholic Church and make ***himself head of his all new Church of England.***

8th March

Today is officially recognised as 'International Women's Day' and is proudly celebrated in many countries around the world. The event was actually started in the United States of America over 110 years ago. ***Three cheers to all women around the world everywhere****.*

8th March

He had floated like a butterfly and stung like a bee through 31 fights had Muhammad Ali - But tonight in 1971 he was was beaten for the first time in his career. Joe Frazier won this epic battle at Madison Square Garden in what ***became known as the 'Fight of the Century'.***

8th March

When Queen Anne ascended to the British throne today in 1702 it looked as if the reign of the Stuart dynasty would prevail forever especially as the Queen would have 17 children but unfortunately for the Stuarts ***all of Anne's children died long before she did.***

9th March

*When the New York Toy Fair took place today in 1959 an all new grown up doll was unveiled to the world and this doll would become one of the most sought after must-haves for millions of children. Named **Barbara Millicent Roberts she is better known as Barbie**.*

9th March

*Tonight in 1945 the U.S. Air Force carried out a devastating fire-bomb attack on Japan killing close to 100,000 mostly civilian people and leaving 1,000,000 homeless. A few weeks later the man who authorised the attack, President F.D **Roosevelt suffered a brain haemorrhage and dropped dead.***

9th March

*A Japanese soldier named Onoda gave himself up to his commanding officer today in 1974 and finally left the Philippine jungle where he'd been waging a one-man war for almost 30 years refusing to believe WWII was over and that **Japan had surrendered 29 years earlier**.*

10th March

*The first Census of Great Britain took place today in 1801 following an Act of Parliament the previous year and has since been carried out every 10 years. When this year's Census is complete the population will be **considerably more than the original count of just ten million.***

10th March

The world's first telephone call took place this morning in 1876 as Alexander Graham Bell demonstrated his invention with the help of his friend Watson. No one was sure quite what to say when answering the telephone until ***Thomas Edison suggested to simply say "Hello".***

10th March

Founded today in 1831 was the French Foreign Legion which forms part of the French military without swearing allegiance to France. Anyone who joins the ranks of the red and green does face severe psychological stress ***but it still boasts around 8,000 members.***

10th March

King Charles I decided he'd put up with enough government meddling into the affairs of his country so today in 1629 the King dissolved parliament and for eleven years the country was under 'Personal Rule'. Perhaps ***he thought to himself - Who needs politicians?***

11th March

English playwright William Shakespeare tells us the wedding of two star-crossed lovers took place today in 1302 and the story was one of romance and tragedy. The blushing bride was just 13 years old her groom was slightly older and ***the happy couple were Romeo & Juliet.***

11th March

The Great Sheffield Flood of 1864 took place today when the brand new Dale Dyke Damn burst its banks while being filled with water. Officials stood on ceremony to declare the damn Open when tragedy struck with the ***loss of over 240 lives and destruction of 600 homes****.*

11th March

Rudolph Höss the evil commandant of death camp Auschwitz was finally arrested today in Germany 1946 where he was posing as a gardener. Höss was beaten with pick axe handles before being dragged away and the final solution ***for him would be his own long overdue execution.***

11th March

The Eternal City of Rome celebrated a major milestone this March day in 1986 and celebrations were aplenty. The city that was founded in 753 BC by Romulus and Remus, famous for gladiatorial combat, its Coliseum and a mighty Empire ***was now 'One Million' days old.***

12th March

When the Beatles took to the stage this evening in 1963 something wasn't quite right, there was Ringo on the drums with George and Paul on guitar and vocals but John was missing due to illness. So for (almost) one night only - ***The Fab Four performed as a Threesome****.*

12th March

At midday today in 1913 Canberra was declared the new capital of Australia but the city didn't actually exist and had to be created. A further 14 years passed before the project was complete and Canberra Day is ***celebrated annually on the 2nd Monday in March.***

12th March

The Year was 1938 and Nazi Germany's Leader had been in office over five years when he decided to make a move into another country today. Hitler knew the world was watching but that wasn't going to stop him so ***he quietly invaded the country of his birth - Austria****.*

12th March

When iconic comic the Beano was published today in 1951 the front cover belonged to Dennis the Menace in his red and black striped sweater. This unforgettable character was a little rascal and along side him everywhere he went ***was his faithful little dog Gnasher.***

13th March

Exotic seductress Mata Hari took to the stage in a Paris theatre this night in 1905 and as the lights went down so did her gown. Naked in the candlelight she stood facing a shocked silent audience. Twelve years later a fully clothed ***Mata was shot dead facing a firing squad.***

13th March

When William Herschel discovered a Planet floating in the sky this March evening in 1781 he decided to name it after King George III. This gas giant orbits the Sun almost on its side with 42 years of Summer 42 of Winter ***and is now known to the world as Uranus****.*

13th March

The shocking Dunblane massacre took place this morning in 1996 when a gunman marched into the Primary School all guns blazing. This killer murdered 16 pupils and a teacher before turning the gun on himself in one of ***the deadliest mass shootings in British history****.*

13th March

When William Herschel spotted the seventh planet from the Sun today in 1781 with his lovely new telescope he decided to name it Georgium Sidus after George III but this planet which takes 84 years to orbit the Sun ***was later renamed after the Greek God of the Sky.***

14th March

*Born in London this March day in 1933 was a boy named Maurice Micklewhite who later became known as the magnificent Sir Michael Caine. This movie icon delivered thousands of lines but none more famous than "****You're only supposed to blow the bloody doors off".***

14th March

Night club boss Jack Ruby was sentenced to death today in 1964 after being convicted of the murder of Lee Harvey Oswald. But his lawyers moved swiftly to have the ruling overturned and the man known as the 'Assassins - Assassin' ***died before the courts could try him again****.*

14th March

Albert Einstein had moved to New Jersey, won a Nobel Prize, been divorced, married his cousin and today in 1951 he celebrated his 72nd birthday. Well known for his famous equation E=mc2 Einstein said his second best invention ***was when he boiled an egg in his soup.***

14th March

Today is recognised across the globe as Pi Day due to the numeric link of 3.14 starting Pi. Mathematicians everywhere will testify that Pi is a wonderful never ending irrational number which makes it the most fascinating number ***in world mathematics 3.1415926535.....***

15th March

The world's first and oldest registered .com domain name on the internet was launched this March day in 1985 and is known as www.symbolics.com This is the one that signalled the start of the internet boom but you have to ***be careful how you pronounce it.***

15th March

He was told "Beware the idea of March" but Julius Caesar marched into the senate in Rome today in 44BC protected by nothing more than his toga. Moments later this fearless leader was brutally killed after ***conspirators led by Marcus Brutus stabbed him 23 times****.*

15th March

When German & American warships faced-off today in 1889 a South Pacific battle was imminent. Then a sudden violent storm struck and smashed the ships into each other destroying six of them proving the might of man ***cannot compare to the force of Mother Nature.***

15th March

When Julius Ceasar was murdered this dark afternoon on the Ides of March in 44 BC he was stabbed 23 times but only one stab wound was fatal. The callous cold-blooded ringleader of the attack, Brutus now hangs ***in the Ninth Circle of Hell alongside Judas Iscariot.***

16th March

A crowd of just over 2,000 attended the first ever FA Cup Final today in 1872 at the Kennington Oval in London to watch Wanderers beat Royal Engineers 1 – 0 thanks to a goal by Morton Betts. The winners then had to wait ***a full month before they received their trophy.***

16th March

Henry Ford created cars in all shapes and sizes and his motor company would assemble and sell almost one million of them every year. When his Fifty Millionth car rolled off the production line this March day in 1958 ***Henry proudly named it the Ford Thunderbird.***

16th March

The Driving Test was introduced for UK Roads today in 1935 and to avoid a mad rush early examinations were voluntary. There wasn't a great deal for a driver to do to achieve driving success and the first person to gain a treasured ***Test Pass was a man named Mr. Beene****.*

16th March

This day in March 1968 was a day of shame for American military during the Vietnam war. Many hundreds of defenceless Vietnamese women and children were attacked and slaughtered by US soldiers in ***the merciless attack known as the My Lai Massacre****.*

17th March

Edward the Black Prince was the son of King Edward III and when he was made Duke of Cornwall today in 1337 the first Dutchy in England was formed. But although this Duke was a King in the making he would ***never live long enough to wear the Crown.***

17th March

This March day in 1995 saw the end of the life of notorious criminal Ronnie Kray as he went to meet his maker. His sentence of life in prison meant the wooden box was the only way out of confinement for Ronnie and he bowed out ***five years before twin brother Reggie.***

17th March

When Saint Patrick died today in 461 AD he left an everlasting legacy and there is a wonderful quote which reads: "May the Irish hills caress you, may her lakes and rivers bless you, may the luck of the Irish enfold you and ***may the blessings of Saint Patrick behold you"****.*

17th March

The Year was 45BC when Roman leader Julius Caesar swept aside the forces of Pompey the Younger this day in March at the bloody Battle of Munda. Although he didn't know it at the time this would be the last battle the ***all conquering Caesar would ever fight.***

18th March

Russian Cosmonaut Alexei Leonov became the first person ever to walk in Space when he did so today in 1965. He nipped out for a bit of fresh air and after ten minutes walking along the wing of his spacecraft gazing at the stars ***he declared "The Earth is Round".***

18th March

Sir Robert Walpole is recognised as the country's first and longest serving Prime Minister holding office for almost twenty one years from 1721 to 1742. Before his untimely death today in 1745 he had served diligently ***under the monarchs George I and George II.***

18th March

Mahatma Ghandi fell foul of British magistrates in India today in 1922 and was sentenced to six years imprisonment for disobedience. This Indian activist was very anti-British and refused to wear anything that was British made ***and that included his famous flip-flops****.*

18th March

It was in Paris 1662 buses took to the streets for the first time today carrying fare paying passengers. This new form of transport was a carriage designed to hold eight people pulled by seven horses but the idea didn't catch on and ***was soon abandoned by the French.***

19th March

An immigrant ship named Monarch of the Seas set sail from Liverpool today in 1866 and its destination was the bright lights of New York City. But within minutes of leaving port tragedy struck and the ship capsized ***sending 738 terrified people to a watery grave.***

19th March

The Upper House of the UK Parliament is the House of Lords but an Act of Parliament which was passed this very afternoon in 1649 during the English Civil War confirmed it's abolishment. The Lords were declared ***- Useless and dangerous to the people of England****.*

19th March

Amidst the English Civil War the House of Lords was abolished this day in 1649 on the orders of the House of Commons and the reason behind the decision was very simple. The House of Lords was declared ***'useless and dangerous to the people of England'.***

19th March

The official opening ceremony of one of the world's most iconic bridges took place this very afternoon in 1932 Australia. Weighing in at 52,000 tons the Sydney Harbour Bridge is held together by 6,000,000 rivets and ***fittingly is nicknamed the Coat-Hanger****.*

20th March

The death of Henry IV this evening in 1413 was karma for some. This King murdered his predecessor and the curse put on him to die a painful death in Jerusalem seemingly came true as his final painful hours were inside ***the Westminster Abbey chamber of Jerusalem.***

20th March

Princess Anne and Mark Phillips got a shock this March afternoon in 1974 when an attempted kidnapping was made on the Princess by crazed gunman Ian Ball. The would be kidnapper told her to get out of the car to which ***the Princess replied "Not bloody likely".***

20th March

It was Fast Food a go-go today in 1930 as Colonel Harland Sanders opened his first Kentucky Fried Chicken outlet to the delight of many. The secret recipe for this Finger Lickin' Chicken is scribbled in pencil on a note and ***still kept in a bank vault in Kentucky.***

20th March

World Cup finals were looming in 1966 when the World Cup was stolen from it's display case just before noon this sunny Sunday. A ransom demand was made and the Sweeney called in but the famous Trophy ***was found one week later by a dog named Pickles****.*

21st March

The notorious Alcatraz high security prison for the criminally insane finally closed its doors today in 1963 and the last 27 prisoners were taken away in chains. Though they do say ***"You can take the Criminal out of Alcatraz but you can't take Alcatraz out of the Criminal".***

21st March

During the reign of Bloody Mary the life of Archbishop of Canterbury Thomas Cranmer was in real danger then today in 1556 the Queen rid herself of this Protestant. Cranmer was taken to the block and his head Chopped off ***but not before he declared the Pope an Antichrist.***

21st March

When Twitter was founded today in 2006 they wanted Tweets kept straight to the point so a limit of 140 characters was the maximum set for a post but that number has since doubled for some.

T.W.I.T.T.E.R = ***Thoughts Which I Think They Enjoy Reading.***

22nd March

Jumbo the Elephant was taken from London Zoo today in 1882 aboard a wagon destined for America. The giant African elephant had been sold to the P.T. Barnum circus and such was his fame Jumbo later became ***the inspiration for the Disney film Dumbo.***

22nd March

Many men have claimed to fly like a bird and none more so than Frenchman Leo Valentin who was born today in 1919 and considered the most famous 'Bird man' of all time. But like other would-be 'Bird men' Valentin ***found out the hard way that Man cannot fly.***

22nd March

*People watched in horror today in 1978 as famous circus family the 'Flying Wallenders' performed a fatal high wire act between two hotels in Puerto Rico. Screams rang out after Karl Wallenda lost his footing on the tightrope **and from ten stories high fell to his death**.*

22nd March

*The highly successful Hollywood movie Forrest Gump tells the tale of many famous events through the eyes of the main character Forrest. Towards the end of the movie Forrest poignantly tells us 22.3.1982 fell on a Saturday **but that day actually fell on a Monday.***

23rd March

*This is quite a day for Olympian Gold Medallists and Record Breakers as Mo Farah, Chris Hoy, Steve Redgrave Sir Roger Bannister all share today as their birthday. So if today's your big day you may want to get into training **'coz you never know what might happen.***

23rd March

*The first of the famous Frost-Nixon interviews took place today in 1977 and more would follow in the coming weeks. Whilst they spelt disaster for Nixon they catapulted the career of Frost who never looked back and regularly said **"Hello, Good Evening and Welcome".***

23rd March

The famous phrase OK was first published today in 1839 in the Boston Morning Post newspaper and it was used as a shortened version of the words 'all correct'. This easy pronunciation caught on very quickly and it ***is now the most used phrase in the world OK****.*

23rd March

US President Herbert Hoover wanted to improve communications with the outside world from his desk. So today in 1929 he ordered a telephone be installed in the Oval Office and if you ever feel the need to call the White House ***then 1-202-456-1111 is the number to ring.***

24th March

A boy named Mark Calaway born today in USA 1965 grew up to be an all-in wrestler and during the WWE heyday this 6'10" giant was a firm favourite. Along with the likes of The Rock and Hulk Hogan the fans always cheered ***for this man they called The Undertaker.***

24th March

A boy named Barrow born this March day in 1909 USA was destined to meet a lady named Parker and once the two met their life of crime was set. Law breakers side by side right until the day they died they could run but couldn't hide ***the notorious Bonnie & Clyde.***

24th March

The reign of the House of Tudor finally ended this March afternoon in 1603 with the passing of Queen Elizabeth I. The Virgin Queen left no heir to the throne so Scotland's Stuart James VI joyfully galloped all the way to London ***to be crowned King James I of England.***

24th March

The Crowns of England and Scotland became one today in 1603 when Scotland's King James VI galloped south to be crowned England's James I. This Stuart King introduced the game of Golf to England and during his reign he ***famously foiled the Gunpowder plot.***

25th March

Today celebrates Independence for Greece commemorating the War of Greek Independence which started exactly 199 years ago. The Battle was bloody and brutal but the Greeks were unrelenting and their cry ***"Freedom or Death" became the motto of the revolution****.*

25th March

A baby girl born this day in Memphis Tennessee 1942 USA became one of the greatest singer songwriters of all time and topped many a music poll. Her name was Aretha Franklyn AKA The Queen of Soul and Aretha sang ***many a fine melody including R.E.S.P.E.C.T.***

25th March

Richard the Lionheart made a fatal mistake today in 1199 when he stepped into the night air in France without wearing his armour. He was struck full in the chest by a bolt from a French crossbow and 12 days later ***this crusading King succumbed to his mortal wound****.*

25th March

John Lennon made global headlines again today in 1969 just days after marrying Yoko Ono. The newly-weds invited the world's press to their 'Bed-In for Peace' at the Hilton Hotel in Amsterdam to promote the start of ***their peaceful protest against the Vietnam war.***

26th March

More people than ever before were able to watch the Aintree Grand National today in 1960 as this famous race was televised for the very first time. Horses thundered along at a furious pace but the one that crossed the line ***and smiled for the cameras first was Merryman II.***

26th March

A great storm broke out tonight in 1827 following the passing of Ludwig Van Beethoven. He was of the greatest composers ever to grace the musical arena even though he lost his hearing in his twenties and it's said ***his last words were "I shall hear in Heaven".***

26th March

The WWII Battle of Iwo Jima had lasted just over a month when it ended today in 1945 and although victory went to Allied American forces the price they paid was high. As well as the 18,000 Japanese lives that were lost ***6,000 American marines*** *also perished.*

27th March

When Charles I ascended to the throne this Spring day in 1625 he became the second Stuart King to take to the throne but his reign was catastrophic. During his 23 years on the throne this King lost a Civil war, lost his Parliament, ***lost the Monarchy and Lost his head.***

27th March

A lady named Mary Mallon was put into quarantine today in New York City 1915 and had to stay there for the rest of her natural life. She was the disease carrying cook who infected other people leading to ***the death of many and history knows her as Typhoid Mary.***

28th March

Following Britain's 'Winter of Discontent' things got even worse for PM James Callaghan when a vote of no confidence in his Government was passed by the House of Commons today in 1979. This would cost James his job ***even though he only lost by one vote.***

28th March

Just to make absolutely sure that everyone across Germany knew all about the Nuremberg Rallies the Nazi party released a propaganda movie this March day in 1935 for everyone to watch and Adolf Hitler was the driving force behind ***the film they called "Triumph of Will".***

29th March

Edward of York defeated forces from the House of Lancaster today in 1461 at Towton in Yorkshire. This is the bloodiest battle ever to take place on English soil and following his victory Edward declared himself King Edward IV and ***the Wars of the Roses were on a break.***

29th March

Three years on from the shocking My Lai Massacre in Vietnam where hundreds of defenceless women and children were slaughtered by US military the man responsible for the onslaught was sentenced to life behind bars today ***after being found Guilty of premeditated murder.***

30th March

Tipperary Tim became the first 100/1 shot to win the Grand National when he galloped past the post today in 1928. Just before the start of the race someone shouted to the jockey that for him to win the other horses would all have to fall ***and those words of wisdom came true.***

30th March

Born this March day in Bradford 1905 was Albert Pierrepoint and he was the Hangman who executed hundreds of criminals. His other job was a publican and he once had a pub in Oldham but no matter what name he gave to his pub ***- The locals always called it The Hangman.***

31st March

The World Wrestling Federation staged the first Wrestlemania event this evening in 1985 and this 'Showcase of Immortals' took place at Madison Square Garden. The main event introduced WWF World Champion ***Hulk Hogan and Mr T and they brought the house down****.*

31st March

When Charlotte Bronté passed away this Spring afternoon in 1855 she was aged just 39 and the eldest of the Bronté sisters. Charlotte left an enduring legacy through her many novels and though her life has gone her ***wonderful works of literature very much live on.***

April

The Month we know as April is taken from the Latin word Aprilis referencing the 'Opening' of Flowers in Spring

April is the First of 4 Months which have just 30 Days and is Famed for Fools Day and Showers

It is widely Acknowledged the Month of April is Named after the Beautiful Greek Goddess Aphrodite

Although April is the Fourth Month of the Year It Is the First Month Alphabetically

The Birthstone for April is the Diamond and the Signs of the Zodiac for this Month are Aries and Taurus

The Month of April once had just 29 Days until Roman Leader Julius Ceasar came along and Gave it the Extra Day

St. George's Day falls on April 23rd Each Year But This Warrior Saint Never Actually Ventured into England

Aphrodite is the Goddess of Sexual Love and Beauty who had a Belt that Caused others to Fall in Love with the Wearer

That's a Fact !!

1st April

This April day in 1891 Chicago Illinois William Wrigley Jr founded the Wrigley company and people all over the world have been chewing their gum ever since. The composition of the gum is synthetic rubber and Wrigley's gum ***was the first product ever to carry a barcode.***

1st April

The RMS Atlantic sank off the coast of Nova Scotia this April day in 1873 with the loss of 547 lives making it one of the worst marine disasters to take place in the 19th century. The ship was operated by White Star Line ***and 39 years later the same company lost Titanic.***

2nd April

The man who helped shape the sound of Motown was born today in 1939 Washington DC and has been an inspiration to many. Known as the Prince of Soul he was the magnificent Marvin Gay but the day before he turned 45 ***Marvin was shot and killed by his own father****.*

2nd April

Four very daring men broke into underground safety deposit boxes in London's Hatton Garden this April day in 2015 and made away with a haul worth a cool £200 million. This unprecedented audacious crime is recognised as the ***Largest burglary in English legal history.***

2nd April

This was a big day in 1800 for Ludwig van Beethoven and an even bigger night as 29 year old German composer lead the premiere of his First Symphony in Vienna. And oh what a show but the maestro could ***barely hear the audience applause as he was almost deaf.***

2nd April

The only horse to win the Aintree Grand National on three separate occasions reached that milestone this afternoon in 1977 and it was Red Rum. Rummy was runner-up the two previous years but was back in front today ***creating his own piece of horse racing history.***

3rd April

Runners and riders were chomping at the bit at the start of today's Grand National in 1993 but red-faced officials messed up. Thirty horses charged off into the distance oblivious to the false start and Esha Ness finished ***ahead of the field in the race that never was.***

3rd April

The Coronation of England's only Saintly King took place today in 1043 at Winchester Cathedral and it was Edward the Confessor who wore the crown. Although the King went on to reign in relative calm for the next ***23 years - when he died all hell broke loose.***

3rd April

It is widely acknowledged King John murdered his nephew Arthur today in 1203 to stop him seizing the English throne. The murder was frowned upon by many but it meant John would reign for further 13 years and during ***that time he signed the historic Magna Carta****.*

4th April

William Henry Harrison was ninth President of the United States but died of pneumonia today in 1841 having held office for just 32 days. His successor was John Tyler who just didn't seem suited to the role and wasn't taken seriously ***so he was soon dubbed - His Accidency.***

4th April

A woman of the night named Emma Smith was brutally murdered in the early hours of this morning in 1888 and she was the first of the 11 unsolved 'Whitechapel Murders'. This gave rise to the Jack the Ripper theory ***but whoever the murderer was they were never ever caught****.*

4th April

When Earth Summit won at Aintree this day in 1998 he became the only horse ever to win the National at three different race courses. This long distance runner had already won the Scottish and Welsh meetings and ***today he galloped into Grand National history.***

5th April

L'Escargot tasted victory at the Grand National today in 1975 after finishing third then second the two previous years. It was the fourth and final appearance at Aintree for this Irish Gelding and this was the day at the Grand National ***when - The Snail beat all the horses.***

5th April

It was this day in Massachusetts 1908 the legendary star of the silver screen Bette Davis was born she was one of the greatest of her age. Bette played unsympathetic characters exceptionally well and was so good at the ***age of 39 she was the highest paid woman in America****.*

5th April

This April afternoon in 1902 an international football match between Scotland and England was underway at Ibrox when disaster struck. A stand collapsed and hundreds of supporters were sent crashing to the concrete below - ***25 people were killed and 500 more were injured.***

6th April

The opening of the first modern Olympic Games was celebrated this Spring day in Athens 1896 after being banned 1,500 years earlier by Roman Emperor Theodosius I. Ever since then the Olympians from Greece have ***lead the way at every Olympic opening ceremony.***

6th April

Playwright and poet Oscar Wilde was arrested this April evening in 1895 after losing a libel case against the Marquess of Queensbury. The trial that followed proved damning for Wilde and when he spoke of ***'The love that dare not speak it's name'*** *things only got worse.*

6th April

The last pre-covid Grand National took place today in 2019 and Tiger Roll cleared the 30 fences and crossed the finish line first to claim his second victory in this great race. There are 16 fences on the course and horses have to ***jump 14 of them twice and 2 of them once.***

6th April

When England's King Richard I succumbed to his chest wound today in 1199 he had ruled for just 10 years. This Lionhearted warrior had spent most of his reign on various crusades far from home and while he was ***on his deathbed in France the Crown passed to King John.***

7th April

The 1997 Grand National was ran this Monday afternoon after the course had been evacuated two days earlier following an IRA bomb threat. It was the first time in 50 years the race was ran on a weekday but ***one horse that didn't mind was winner Lord Gyllene.***

7th April

Born today in 1915 Philadelphia was the magnificent Jazz and Swing singer Billie Holiday who rose to fame at an early age performing in Harlem. Her short life was ruined by drug abuse and this wonderful performer left us with ***her poignant album - Lady Sings The Blues****.*

7th April

The fastest winning time in the Aintree Grand National steeplechase was clocked today in 1990 at 8 minutes 47 seconds and the winning horse was Mr Frisk. Off like a shot from a gun he couldn't be caught as he galloped ***around the course faster than any other horse****.*

8th April

Las Vegas opened a new attraction this April morning in 1999 and even by their standards this was quite unbelievable. They unveiled a $1.2 billion dollar replica of the world's most famous passenger liner RMS Titanic and ***next to the great ship they put a great big Iceberg****.*

8th April

Eight members of Motorcycle gang known as the Bandidos No Surrender Crew were slaughtered today in 2006 in Ontario Canada. A rival gang had called the Bandidos Winnipeg Chapter had carried out the gang killings ***which became known as the Shedden Massacre.***

8th April

The 100/1 outsider Foinavon claimed his famous victory at the Grand National today in 1967 after avoiding a Melee 23 fences in. There have been five 100/1 Grand National winners but Foinavon remains the only one of them ***to have a fence named in his honour.***

8th April

I wonder if one day that, you'll say that, you care if you say you love me madly, I'll gladly, be there like a Puppet on a String...........Sandy Shaw topped the lot at the Eurovision Song Contest this evening in 1967 with her ***winning wonder song - Puppet on a String.***

9th April

It was today in 1942 that 75,000 American and Philippine defenders on Bataan were forced to surrender to Japanese troops and their lives were in peril. They were force walked 60 miles and along the way thousands ***died or were slaughtered on this Bataan Death March****.*

9th April

After four years of bloodshed the American civil war finally came to an end this April day in 1865 when the confederates decided it was time to surrender. Abraham Lincoln could finally look to the future but unfortunately ***for Lincoln his life would only last another 5 days****.*

9th April

*Supersonic passenger jet plane Concorde made its first UK test flight this April afternoon in 1969 as it roared off the Fulton runway into blue skies above Bristol wowing the crowds. The Concorde captain piloting this **famous flight was Brian Trubshaw from Liverpool.***

10th April

*It was this night in 1955 that a lady named Ruth Ellis stood outside a London pub, pulled a shotgun from her handbag then aimed at her abusive lover and pulled the trigger. After firing until there were no bullets left **Ruth calmly gave herself up to an off-duty policeman.***

10th April

*A strange looking food appeared in London this afternoon in 1633 and they called it Plantaine fruit. People thought it was oddly shaped but as it became popular the apples & oranges took a front seat at the back and people **could now say - Oh yes we have some Bananas.***

10th April

*The writing had been on the wall in the music world for some time when Paul McCartney announced today in 1970 he was leaving the Beatles. This is the day the Fab-Four split up but it seemed no matter what official **reasons were given everyone still blames Yoko Ono.***

10th April

As Titanic set sail for the Big Apple this April afternoon in 1912 thousands of people waved her away from the dockside. The Great ship would never reach her destination but as she left Southampton dock she very nearly ***collided with a smaller ship named New York.***

11th April

The centuries old historic Stone of Scone on which Scottish monarchs had sat for their Coronation throughout the ages was found today in 1951 in Arbroath Abbey. The Stone had been taken from Westminster Abbey by ***Scottish students determined to return it to Scotland.***

11th April

The Coronation of William III and his wife Mary II took place today in 1689 and for the first time ever in Great Britain two people reigned as joint sovereigns. Between them they reigned for the next thirteen years and ***in case you were wondering - William outlived Mary.***

11th April

It was lift-off for Apollo 13 today in 1970 and of the 7 Apollo Moon landing missions this is the unlucky one that didn't reach its destiny. The captain said "Houston we have a problem" but the crew were able to rectify ***their tricky situation to avoid being lost in space****.*

12th April

When Russian Cosmonaut Yuri Gagarin became first man in space today in 1961 aboard Vostok 1 it was much to the annoyance of the Americans. Russia were winning the space race and the only way USA could get ***ahead of them was if they put a man on the Moon****.*

12th April

The Year was 1992 and the long awaited, much anticipated grand opening of Euro Disneyland finally took place today and the park was packed out. Before long Disney had a re-think about the name and going along with ***public opinion it was re-named Disneyland Paris.***

12th April

The collapse of the Broughton Suspension bridge in Manchester England today in 1831 was caused by soldiers marching across it's surface. The British Army looked into the matter and with a stiff upper lip ***ordered all soldiers to break-step when crossing a bridge****.*

12th April

Franklyn Delano Roosevelt is the only American President ever voted into office for four consecutive terms. While sitting at his desk posing for his portrait today in 1945 Franklyn felt unwell and breathing his last breath ***he suddenly left America needing a new President.***

13th April

Born today in 1743 was Thomas Jefferson who became the third President of America and the man who wrote the Declaration of Independence. Of the 56 men who signed this famous document no less than 8 of them ***had actually been born in Britain****.*

13th April

Exactly 200 years after his birth the Thomas Jefferson Memorial was unveiled today in 1943 in honour of their 3rd President and the man who wrote the Declaration of Independence. The memorial stands proud in Washington DC ***and today in the USA is Jefferson Day.***

13th April

Born this Spring morning in 1866 was one half of the world's most infamous Wild West duo and his name was Butch Cassidy. He and his partner the Sundance Kid made their living by holding up trains and banks at gunpoint ***and both would die in a bloody shootout****.*

13th April

Knowing they were now facing defeat in WWII German troops got together this April morning in 1945 to commit yet another despicable war crime. They rounded up 1,000 political and military prisoners in a place called ***Gardelegen and mercilessly murdered all of them.***

14th April

A gunfight took place this afternoon in 1881 outside a courthouse in El Paso Texas and 4 men bit the dust. At the centre of the commotion a Marshall named Dallas Stoudenmire who killed 3 men and was so fast that this is ***known as the 'Four Dead in Five Seconds' Gunfight.***

14th April

The Wars of the Roses produced many bloody battles and one took place this Easter Sunday in 1471 when Yorkists defeated Lancastrians at the Battle of Barnet. This battle saw the murder of Richard Neville aka Warwick ***the Kingmaker as his skull was crushed with an axe****.*

14th April

German U-Boat U-1206 was in the North Sea near Peterhead today in the final year of WWII when it suffered a toilet malfunction. Those who were able to escape the Sinking Sub were captured by British battleships on ***the surface and taken as prisoners of war.***

14th April

Abraham Lincoln signed a document today in 1865 authorising the formation of a Secret Service to protect the President. The same evening Lincoln was sitting with his wife in the Ford Theatre enjoying a comedy show when ***an assassin shot him at point-blank range.***

15th April

Millions were enjoying Live from Her Majesty's on TV tonight in 1984 when funny-man Tommy Cooper suddenly collapsed then died on stage. Those watching thought it was part of the act and host Jimmy Tarbuck later commented ***"Tommy's final act fooled Everyone".***

15th April

Unbeaten since winning the FIFA World Cup England played the Auld Enemy at Wembley this afternoon in 1967 and were overwhelming favourites to win the match but the Scots had other ideas and totally dominated the game with ***the final score England 2 – 3 Scotland.***

15th April

The tragic events of this Saturday afternoon at Hillsborough in 1989 are well known by the people of Liverpool and all those involved with the Football Club. Authorities, police and segments of the press lied about the 96 who died ***but they couldn't cover up the truth forever.***

15th April

It was in the early hours of this morning the great ship Titanic sank without trace in the freezing cold waters of the Atlantic Ocean after hitting an iceberg. Over 1,500 people lost their lives and the world was in shock ***when the unthinkable happened to the unsinkable.***

15th April

The world famous Norte-Dame de Paris which had taken the French almost 200 years to build to completion was set ablaze today in 2019 and the cathedral suffered serious damage. The French rallied and soon started ***restoration work to bring back 'Our Lady of Paris'.***

16th April

As many as 1,000 Jewish Zealots held up in their fortress had kept Roman warriors at bay until this April day in 73 AD when the enemy finally broke through. But all the Romans found were 2 women and 3 children ***everyone else had committed mass suicide at Masada.***

16th April

The Battle of Culloden took place this morning in 1746 as Bonnie Prince Charlie and his Jacobite army made one final attempt to seize the British throne from the House of Hanover but the Jacobites were destroyed and the ***Stuart claim to the crown was gone forever.***

16th April

Born today in 1889 was Charlie Chaplin the star of silent movies both sides of the Atlantic. At the height of his stardom the actor entered a Charlie Chaplin 'look-a-like' competition but his impersonation of himself was ***only good enough to earn him third place.***

16th April

Rudolph Hoss was one of Nazi Germany's most evil commandants and his crimes finally caught up with him following the Nuremberg trials. Hoss was the mass murderer who ran Death Camp Auschwitz so he was taken ***back there today in 1947 and then executed.***

17th April

American founding father and man of many talents Benjamin Franklyn bowed out today in 1790 after quite a colourful life. Well known for humour and wit Benjamin was not allowed to contribute to the Declaration of ***Independence in case he put a joke in it.***

17th April

Benjamin Franklyn was one of America's Founding Fathers and the man who discovered Electricity. He was also a humorist and when died today in 1790 he had arranged for a message on his headstone to read ***Here lies Benjamin Franklyn - Food for Worms.***

17th April

The Bay of Pigs invasion started today in 1961 as a group of Cuban exiles attempted to overthrow Fidel Castro. The perpetrators had been financed by the US government and trained by the CIA but were no match for Castro's men ***and JFK would have to wait another day.***

17th April

This was the morning in 1984 young WPC Yvonne Fletcher of the Metropolitan Police force was fatally wounded by a single gunshot fired from a window on the 1st floor of the Libyan Embassy London. Sadly, to this day ***no-one has ever been convicted of her murder.***

18th April

A devastating and deadly natural phenomenon struck the very heart of San Francisco California very early this morning in 1906. The catastrophic event destroyed most of the city, claimed over 3,000 lives and is remembered as ***The Great San Francisco Earthquake.***

18th April

The largest naval battle since WWII got under way today in 1988 when the United States Armed Forces attacked Iranian Naval Forces in retaliation to their mining of the Persian Gulf. The Americans overwhelmed Iran ***in what is known as Operation Praying Mantis****.*

18th April

Thousands watched RMS Carpathia sail into New York harbour this April day in 1912. Her cargo included 705 very weary passengers, most of whom were survivors of RMS Titanic which had sank three days earlier in ***the freezing cold waters of the Atlantic Ocean.***

19th April

Sir Francis Drake sailed into the main Port of Spain this April day in 1587 and unleashed a terror attack on her anchored ships setting them on fire and sinking any hopes of an attack on England. This single act by 'El Draco' ***delayed the Spanish Armada by a full year****.*

19th April

A couple named Bart and Marge made their TV debut this evening in 1987 when they appeared on the Tracey Ullman show. The Simpsons had arrived and they would soon have their own TV schedule but this introduction to viewers ***was a little sketch entitled Good Night.***

19th April

The deadly 51 day FBI siege of the Branch Davidian building in Waco Texas USA ended in tragedy today in 1993 after a fire broke out. When the smoke finally settled the blaze had caused the death of 76 Davidians which ***included 18 children under the age of ten.***

19th April

The wonderfully vivacious Mae West who became rather famous for her sexual independence and provocative one-liners was sentenced to 10 days imprisonment today in 1927 for staging her play ***Sex****. But her time spent behind bars* ***just served to enhance her notoriety.***

20th April

This was a cold, wet, rain drenched Easter Saturday evening in 1889 when a baby boy was born in Austria. He grew up and fought in WWI then acquired German citizenship and was leader of the Nazi party when he started WWII ***the personification of Evil Adolf Hitler.***

20th April

The American War of Independence had been raging for two days and two bloody battles had already been fought when the Siege of Boston started today in 1775. The Americans did seem fond of Boston particularly as ***they had a 'Tea Party' there 16 months earlier.***

20th April

When Enoch Powell addressed party members this afternoon in 1968 he gave a speech so controversial it caused a political storm and cost him his place in the Shadow Cabinet. Although Enoch called it his Birmingham speech it is ***more widely known as the 'Rivers of Blood'****.*

20th April

In the skies above the Somme today in 1918 Manfred Von Richthofen shot down the last two of the 80 planes he had sent crashing to the ground. Manfred was the Red Baron who terrorised the skies in his red Fokker ***but the following morning he himself was shot down.***

21st April

At 9:30 am this April morning in 1960 Brasilia was declared Capital City of Brazil. The 3 Powers of the Republic were transferred from Rio de Janeiro which had been the Capital for almost 200 years but Brasilia was ***better placed and had been built especially for the job****.*

21st April

Born this April day in London 1926 was princess Elizabeth Alexandra Mary Windsor and at the age of just 25 this Princess became our Queen. And of the country's Kings and Queens there has ever been Elizabeth II is by far ***the longest reigning monarch we've ever seen****.*

21st April

This is a right Royal day of celebration as we say Happy Birthday to Queen Elizabeth II who was born this day in 1926 and is Britain's longest reigning monarch. This same day in 1509 a young Tudor prince ascended to ***the English throne to become King Henry VIII.***

22nd April

The America government passed the 'Coinage Act' today in 1864 with a mandate that all future coins minted in the U.S. would carry the inscription ***In God We Trust****. The words were later made famous in a Hollywood remake of the* ***much loved Miracle on 34th Street.***

22nd April

When a Portuguese explorer named Pedro discovered Brazil today in 1500 he claimed it for the Portuguese Empire. Known as 'Land of the Holy Cross' Brazil is the largest country in South America with one of the most multicultural and ***ethnically diverse nations in the world.***

22nd April

Earth day is celebrated each year on this day when people across the globe show support for environment protection. When it all started today in 1970 over 20 million people poured onto the streets across America in ***the largest 1-day peaceful protest in human history.***

23rd April

The 25 year old King Edmund II also known as Edmund Ironside ascended to the English throne today in 1016 but the young King's reign lasted just 7 months and 7 days. There are many theories as to the cause of ***his death and it is highly likely he was murdered.***

23rd April

King Edward III declared George as England's patron Saint since the warrior had embodied all the characteristics Edward needed to drive England's power and strength. Today was chosen for St George as it was the day of ***his execution in 303 AD in present day Turkey.***

23rd April

When the Coronation of Charles II took place this April day in 1661 thousands of cheering people lined the streets to witness the King being crowned. The country had waited 12 years for the restoration of the monarchy and ***very fittingly Charles chose St George's day.***

24th April

The opening of the Woolworth skyscraper in New York took place today in 1913 and at the time was the tallest building in the world. Such was the 'Wonder of Woollies' stores opened across the world and the ***first Woolworth store to open in the UK was in Liverpool.***

24th April

The Russians had been enjoying themselves in the space race against the USA until today in 1967 when a mission proved fatal. Cosmonaut Vladimir Komarov died aboard Soyuz 1 when its parachute failed to open and ***he became the first human to die during a space mission.***

24th April

Winston Churchill finally received his Knighthood from Her Majesty Queen Elizabeth II today in 1953 He had previously turned down the Order of the Garter having been removed from office in the General Election but he ***would still serve another term as the country's PM****.*

25th April

Born today in 1284 was Edward of Caernarfon who became the first ever English Prince of Wales later ascending to the English throne as King Edward II. He was never the warrior King his father was and his wife Isabella ***made sure he was murdered by her henchmen.***

25th April

A deadly earthquake struck Nepal minutes before noon today in 2015 causing the deaths of almost 9,000 people with 22,000 more injured. Hundreds of thousands of people were made homeless and 22 people also died in ***an avalanche caused by the quake on Mount Everest.***

25th April

Born this April day in 1599 was the man who's Roundheads defeated the King's Cavaliers in the English civil war. He was Oliver Cromwell and as the country's Lord Protector he put a stop to many traditional Christian celebrations and ***Oliver Cromwell even banned Christmas.***

26th April

TV presenter Jill Dando was shot and killed in broad daylight today in 1999 on the doorstep of her London home. The man found guilty and sentenced for this shocking crime was later released on appeal and to this day ***whoever murdered Jill Dando still walks free.***

26th April

When Marvel studios released Avengers Endgame for the watching world to see this day in 2019 it became a blockbuster like no other. Movie-goers turned out in their thousands and the big bucks rolled in making this ***Superhero film the highest grossing movie of all time****.*

26th April

The last person to be held prisoner in Spandau Prison was Rudolph Hess and it was today in April 1894 this Nazi had been born. Hess was Hitler's right hand man when he climbed into a plane and flew to Scotland where he was ***arrested and after a trial sent to Spandau.***

27th April

It was on this sunny afternoon in 1974 when a group of over 10,000 people marched on Washington DC demanding the impeachment of President Richard Nixon over the Whitehouse scandal. Nixon was never impeached ***but he did resign from office later that same year****.*

27th April

Ulysses S. Grant, the 18th American President was born today in 1822 and before his presidential days he led the Union army to victory in the American civil war. Grant served two full Presidential terms and was rather unfairly ***labelled 'Brilliant General - Terrible President'.***

27th April

The first battle in the Scottish War of Independence started today in 1296 and lasted 5 days as Edward I sought to establish authority over the Scots. The wars were caused by English Kings trying to rule in Scotland while ***the Scots just wanted the English to stay in England.***

28th April

It was on the high seas today in 1789 that Mutiny on the Bounty took place and Captain Blyth with 18 others were abandoned in the Pacific Ocean. When the Captain made it back to England the ship Pandora was launched to ***track down Fletcher Christian and his mutineers.***

28th April

Pink Floyd's Dark Side of the Moon which had been recorded in Abbey Road studios topped the US Billboard album charts today in 1973 and stayed in the charts for a record breaking 741 weeks. Which is more than enough ***time to fly to the Dark Side of the Moon and back.***

28th April

The first Wembley FA Cup Final took place this afternoon in 1923 and a packed stadium saw 2 goals scored as Bolton triumphed over West Ham. A policeman riding his horse on the pitch that day to help with crowd control meant ***the game was dubbed - The White Horse Final.***

29th April

The wedding of Prince William and Kate Middleton took place today in 2011 and the loving couple enjoyed a right Royal Banquet. In 1945 another wedding took place this same day and the loving couple who tied the knot ***on that sunny day were Adolph and Eva - Oops !!***

29th April

When 6 days of fighting ended today in Dublin 1916 it meant the Easter Rising was over. Irish rebel leaders who had challenged British rule had little choice but surrender to the overwhelming force against them and ***within a few weeks 16 of their leaders were executed.***

29th April

A wedding took place in a WWII bunker today in 1945, the groom was 55 and his blushing bride was 33 but this was no ordinary wedding. He was Adolf Hitler she was Eva Braun and within just 24 hours the lives of these ***two newly-weds came to a suicidal end.***

30th April

After 11 years in operation Nevada's Boulder Dam was officially re-named this April morning in 1947 to Hoover Dam after the President of the same name. There were plenty of protests about the change but they fell on ***deaf ears and today the name remains the same.***

30th April

It was this April afternoon in 1871 American soldiers attacked and slaughtered Pinal and Aravaipa Apaches by the San Pedro River in Arizona. The apaches had surrendered to the US Army but that didn't stop this bloody assault ***known as the Camp Grant massacre.***

30th April

After declaring independence three years earlier it was today in 1789 America appointed their first President and his name was George Washington who had ran for office completely unopposed. During his 8 years at the top ***George never once took a salary for the job****.*

May

This Fifth Month of the Year is Named after Maia the Roman Goddess of Fertility and Plants

The beginning of May falls in the Spring of the Northern Hemisphere and the Autumn of the Southern Hemisphere

No Other Month In Any Year Starts or Finishes on the Same Days of the Week That Start and Finish the Month of May

When the Month of May Starts on a Friday there will always be Five Fridays, Five Saturdays and Five Sundays

May always has 31 Days giving it 744 Hours and is one of the Longest Months of the Year but has the Shortest Name

The Gemstone for the Month of May is The Emerald and The Zodiac Signs are Taurus and Gemini

This Month was once considered to be Unlucky and a Poem Points out "Marry in May and you'll Rue the Day"

There's a Merry Little Tune that goes "Here we go gathering Nuts in May" – Except There Are No Nuts in May

That's a Fact !!

1st May

This day in 1947 a young lady named Evelyn McHale went to floor 86 of the Empire State Building and jumped to her death. Her lifeless body smashed onto the roof of a parked limousine in the moment of human tragedy that ***became known as the most Beautiful Suicide.***

1st May

New York's Empire State Building was opened today in 1931 by President Herbert Hoover. This iconic structure which has 103 floors stands 1250ft tall and weighs in at 365,000 tons with 6,500 windows that have to be cleaned ***and is held together with 10,000,000 bricks.***

1st May

When the Treaty of Edinburgh-Northampton was signed this May Day in 1328 it meant the Wars of Scottish Independence were finally over. The term War of Independence didn't exist at the time but was added many years ***later after the Americans made it fashionable.***

2nd May

The Queen of England and second wife of Henry VIII was arrested today in 1536 on orders from the King. Her name was Anne Boleyn and she found herself facing charges of adultery, incest, treason and witchcraft while ***her husband already had his eye on his next wife****.*

2nd May

The creator of the magnificent 'Mona Lisa' portrait Leonardo Da Vinci lived until this day in 1519 when he died in the arms of French King Francis I. Da Vinci's famous masterpiece adorns the Paris Louvre museum and ***Mona Lisa has no eyebrows and no eyelashes.***

2nd May

Arnold Dorsey was born today in 1936 and grew up to become a singer but decided he needed a catchy name. Having quite fancied the name of the Russian Composer who wrote the Hansel and Gretel Opera he went with that ***and called himself Englebert Humperdinck.***

3rd May

3rd May Bistritz 8.35pm are first words of Bram Stoker's gothic novel which spawned many films and tells the fortunes of blood sucking Vampire Count Dracula from Transylvania. If you can't sleep at night and can't see ***your reflection in the mirror you must be a vampire.***

3rd May

The most famous horse ever to win the Aintree Grand National steeple chase was born today in 1965 and was named Red Rum. This horse was trained by Ginger McCain and is the only ever 3 x Winner of the Great race and ***Red Rum spelt backwards reads MURDER.***

3rd May

Born this sunny day in 1903 USA was Bing Crosby the singer, dancer and entertainer who was voted 'most admired man alive' at the age of 45 in America. Bing famously sang White Christmas and his legendary radio shows ***gave people a chance to sing-along-a-Bing.***

4th May

Since the Royal Canadian Navy was founded today in 1910 they have barely set a foot out of water. This Naval force of Canada has served with great gusto in the First and Second World Wars the Korean War, the Gulf War, ***the War in Afghanistan and many NATO operations****.*

4th May

The Epsom Derby is Britain's richest Horse Race and it all started today in 1780 when a colt named Diomed was 1st past the winning post. The Derby is the Blue Riband of the turf and the race is now run each year in June as ***part of the Triple Crown in this Sport of Kings.***

4th May

Hollywood icon Audrey Hepburn was born this day in Berlin 1929 and at a young age wanted to star on the silver screen. She became part of Hollywood's Golden Age and one of her most memorable movies was Breakfast at Tiffany's ***where she played call girl Holly Golightly.***

5th May

Iconic fashion designer Coco Chanel chose this particular day in 1921 to launch the world's first modern perfume naming it Chanel No5. This unmistakable fragrance went global when Hollywood goddess Marilyn Monroe ***said Chanel No:5 was all she wore in bed.***

5th May

This day in May 1821 Napoleon Bonaparte breathed his final breath and was later buried in Saint Helena. The death of Napoleon caused much controversy as many believe he was poisoned but the dead Emperor waited ***19 years before receiving his State Funeral.***

5th May

Bobby Sands was a member of the IRA who was arrested after a gun battle in Northern Ireland and sentenced to 14 years imprisonment. He famously led a hunger strike in Maze prison and today in 1981 on Day 66 of ***his hunger strike the prisoner joined the 27 club****.*

5th May

Born this day in May 32 years ago was a baby girl who became a singing superstar before the age of 20 and her name is Adele Adkins. Known to the world as Adele her first 3 albums are named according to her age at ***time of release and collectively add up to 65.***

6th May

Athletes could only dream of running the four-minute mile and although many had tried just as many had failed. That was until this May day in 1954 when Englishman Roger Banister sensationally ran into the record books ***running the mile in 3 minutes 59 seconds.***

6th May

Moors Murderers Myra Hindley and Ian Brady were locked up for life today in 1966 after murdering 5 children. This was 6 months after the death penalty was abolished in the UK so both were kept behind bars until their death with ***Hindley labelled 'most evil woman in Britain'****.*

6th May

King George V ascended to the British throne this day in 1910 following the passing of his father Edward VII and a few years later the King changed the Royal name from Saxe-Coberg Gotha to Windsor. So ***the Royal family are actually named after a building****.*

6th May

Terror struck today in 1937 as Zeppelin airship 'Hindenburg' burst into flames while preparing to land in New Jersey. There were many theories as to the cause of the disaster but Adolf Hitler refused to accept it may ***have been sabotage claiming it was an Act of God.***

7th May

Today in 1915 the Cunard ocean liner RMS Lusitania en route to Liverpool sank after being torpedoed by German U-Boat U-20 with the loss of 1,198 lives. The explosion was too great for one torpedo and speculation ***still surrounds the true contents of the ships cargo****.*

7th May

Three McDonalds employees were murdered today in 1992 during a botched robbery when they were viciously attacked at a restaurant in Sydney Nova Scotia. Another employee managed to survive but was permanently disabled ***in the first 'fast-food' murder in Canada****.*

7th May

When the Lusitania was torpedoed and sank today in 1915 en route to Liverpool during WWI the American people were up in arms as many of the lives lost were their kinfolk. But as angry they were it was another 2 years ***before America joined The Great War****.*

7th May

A baby girl born this May morning in Argentina 1919 grew up to become Argentina's most fascinating First Lady and one of the most famous women in the world. Her name was Eva Perón and she is remembered ***across the globe in book, theatre and film as Evita.***

*8th **May***

*Today in 1945 was a day saw of the formal acceptance by the Allies of Nazi Germany's unconditional surrender of its armed forces ending WWII in Europe. The Instrument of Surrender would soon be signed and this **truly momentous day became known as V.E. Day.***

*8th **May***

*The Siege of Orleons ended today in 1429 after almost 7 months of bloodshed and the French claimed a crushing victory over the English. This was the first time France had won a major battle in the Hundred Years War and it was **all thanks to a young girl named Joan of Arc.***

*8th **May***

*Two French war heroes wanting to make history today in 1927 decided to fly none stop across the Atlantic from Paris to New York. They got themselves ready to go, started the engine and then took off in The White Bird **biplane but the men were never seen again**.*

*8th **May***

*Born this sunny day in 1884 on a farm in Missouri was a boy named Harry Truman and he became America's 33rd President. He thought his name a bit plain so added the S and after giving the order to drop the atom bomb **a plaque on his desk read - The Buck Stops Here**.*

9th May

The oldest alliance in the world is shared between the UK and Portugal and known as the Treaty of Windsor. This treaty was signed and sealed today in 1386 when both countries agreed never to wage war against each other ***directly or indirectly - and they never have.***

9th May

Alfred Hitchcock released Vertigo today in 1958 starring James Stewart and Kim Novak. The movie received mixed reviews at the time but has since been recognised as a true masterpiece of cinema and in 2012 ***replaced Citizen Kane as the greatest film ever made.***

9th May

A man named Thomas Blood walked into the Tower of London today in 1671 disguised as a clergyman and tried to steal the Crown Jewels. He was caught and questioned by Charles II who may have told Blood only the Queen ***was allowed to touch the King's Crown Jewels.***

9th May

In a sign of things to come Friends of the Earth gathered up 1,500 empty bottles this day in 1971 and returned them all to Schweppes. Even though every bottle was clearly stamped none returnable the drinks giant ***had little choice but to accept every single one of them.***

10th May

Winston Churchill had held the office of Prime Minister exactly one year today in 1941 when Rudolph Hess landed his plane in Scotland. The Nazi was quickly arrested then thrown into the Tower of London before being ***sent to spend the rest of his days in Spandau Prison****.*

10th May

The Year was 1940 and the British government needed a strong leader at the helm if they were to defeat the Nazis in WWII but PM Neville Chamberlain wasn't that man. Parliament knew only one man could turn ***the 'V' into Victory - Step forward Winston Churchill.***

10th May

Two Assassins were born this day in May exactly 117 years apart in the USA. The first is John Wilkes Booth born 1838 who shot and killed Abraham Lincoln in Washington DC and the other is Mark Chapman born 1955 ***who shot and killed John Lennon in New York City.***

10th May

This was the day in 1508 Italian sculptor Michelangelo started work on his masterpiece on the ceiling of the Sistine Chapel in the Vatican. This magnificent work of art took over 4 years to complete and the genius ***annoyed the Pope when he gave Adam a belly button.***

11th May

On this late afternoon in 1812 the only ever assassination of a British Prime Minister took place. He was Spencer Percival who's life ended with a bullet from a gun within the House of Commons corridors and as the PM ***collapsed to the floor he shouted - Murder Murder.***

11th May

World Chess Champion Garry Kasparov had a re-match against chess-playing supercomputer Deep Blue today in 1997 following his victory the previous year. This time though Deep Blue was faster than the Master who ***did not like hearing a computer say Check-mate.***

11th May

It was today in 1985 during the last home game of the season that disaster struck at Bradford City Valley Parade football ground. Within minutes a small fire had spread into a ferocious blaze engulfing the main wooden stand ***and 56 lives were lost in this terrible tragedy.***

11th May

An Aberdeen built ship that had left Belfast over a month earlier and bound for Quebec was struck on the starboard by ice toady in 1833 and sank with the loss of up to 265 passengers and crew. The name of this ship that ***sailed the seas to disaster was - Lady of the Lake.***

12th May

Born today in Connecticut 1907 was a baby girl who became a true star of the Silver Screen. The legendary Katherine Hepburn holds the record of 4 Academy Awards for Best Actress and is recognised with good reason ***as the greatest female star of classic Hollywood****.*

12th May

This should have been Coronation Day for King Edward VIII today in 1937 but this King had abdicated the throne and gone off to marry American divorcee Wallis Simpson instead. The Coronation still went ahead as planned ***but the King who was crowned was George VI****.*

12th May

Born today in 1820 and named after the city of her birth was British nurse Florence Nightingale aka The Lady with the Lamp. Her work during the Crimean War changed the face of nursing forever and in memory of Florence ***today is International Nursing Day.***

12th May

Born today in 1945 was Englishman Alan Ball who became one of football's finest and an Everton icon as part of the famous Goodison Holy Trinity. At the age of just 21 Alan was the youngest player on the Wembley pitch ***when England won the 1966 World Cup.***

13th May

Forces loyal to the deposed Mary Queen of Scots were crushed by Scottish Protestants today in 1568 at the Battle of Langside. The victors were lead by the Earl of Moray James Stewart, who was not only a ***sworn enemy of Mary but also her half-brother.***

13th May

The attempt on the life of Pope John Paul II took place today in 1981 when an assassin's bullet struck the pontiff as he entered St. Peter's Square Vatican City. The Pontiff recovered from the shooting and his mode of transport ***was changed to the bulletproof Popemobile.***

13th May

Almost 800 criminals in England were marched in chains today in 1787 and forced aboard anchored ships which took them away to a far off land. The prisoners had been convicted of various crimes and punishment ***for them would be imprisonment in Australia.***

13th May

It was this day in May 1950 the Formula One drivers championship became a reality as the first race ever to take place got under way at Silverstone. Drivers may choose an unassigned number from 2 - 99 under which to drive ***but the No:1 Is always reserved for the Winner.***

14th May

Trouble broke out tonight in Manchester City Centre 2008 between Glasgow Rangers supporters, Zenit supporters and the police when thousands of ticketless fans converged. Police officers were injured and ***39 arrests were made in the Battle of Piccadilly Gardens****.*

14th May

The bloody Battle of Lewes took place today in 1264 when Simon de Montford defeated the forces of English King Henry III. The King was captured by De Montford and held prisoner in the Tower of London where he stayed ***until his son Edward rescued him a year later.***

14th May

A boy born today in 1984 grew up, went to Harvard and with some friends founded the social network site Facebook. The site has so many members that over one million accounts belong to dead people and if you ***use Facebook you can't block Mark Zuckerberg.***

14th May

The Grand opening of an iconic North West's structure took place this sunny afternoon in 1894 and crowds were in awe of Blackpool Tower. This monument stands 518ft tall was built using five million Accrington bricks ***and has a time capsule in its foundations.***

15th May

The second wife of King Henry VIII and mother of the future Elizabeth I stood in the dock today in 1536 facing charges of treason, adultery and incest. The young Queen was very much alone in a room full of hate and ***all she could do was pray to God and await her fate.***

15th May

The Soviets launched Sputnik 3 today in 1958 to go back into Space. Then on the same day 2 years later Sputnik 4 was launched but never re-orbited leading to the conspiracy theory of 'The Lost Cosmonauts' and Space is a ***strange place where no-one can hear you scream****.*

15th May

Although King George III reigned longer than any other British King his reign almost ended today in 1800 when he faced two separate assassination attempts. Lady Luck was on his side as he survived both attacks and went on ***to reign for another twenty years.***

16th May

America's first Academy Awards ceremony took place this evening in 1929 as Hollywood's elite gave themselves a party and Wings won best Movie. When the statuettes were being made a lady remarked that they looked like her Uncle Oscar ***and so the Oscars were born****.*

16th May

Sir Thomas More resigned his post as Lord Chancellor today in 1532 during the reign of Henry VIII which wasn't a good move to make. The knives were out, the vultures were circling and Thomas knew very well that ***sooner or later hell itself would be heading his way.***

16th May

Joan of Arc was canonised by the Pope today in 1920 almost 500 years after the French had burned her to death at the stake. Joan had single handedly changed the fortunes of France in the Hundred Years War but ***they executed their Maid of Orleóns for Heresy.***

16th May

Marie Antoinette was 14 when she married 15 year old Louis Auguste today in 1770 and they were very happy. He became King Louis XVI and she became his Queen but when they lost their heads during the French Revolution ***he went quietly - she went kicking and screaming.***

17th May

The Wonderful Wizard of Oz published today in 1900 was so good it was later turned into a must-see family movie. Dorothy went singing and dancing along the Yellow Brick Road wearing Silver slippers in the book but ***in the movie they became a magical Ruby Red.***

17th May

L. Frank Baum's novel 'The Wonderful Wizard of Oz' was published today in 1900 long before it was ever made into a movie. Frank never lived long enough to see his story on the big screen but he did present the very ***first copy of his famous book to his little sister.***

17th May

It was another bloody day at the Tower in 1536 during the reign of King Henry VIII when George Boleyn along with 5 other men were convicted of treason and had their heads chopped off . Inside the Tower George's ***sister Anne Boleyn awaited a similar fate.***

17th May

Almost 300 years after Columbus discovered America, it was this morning in 1792 that the New York stock exchange finally opened for business. Standing in Wall Street Lower Manhattan and nicknamed the The Big Board this is ***the largest stock exchange in the world.***

18th May

The Royal Wedding of the future King Henry II of England and Eleanor of Aquitaine took place this sunny afternoon in 1152 and together they stayed. But the wedded bliss didn't last long and Henry later locked Eleanor ***inside the Tower of London for almost sixteen years.***

18th May

Mount St Helens in the Washington State erupted today in 1980 and although the authorities knew she was going to blow they severely misjudged the intensity and direction. The wrong safety advice was given to the public ***and 57 lives were tragically lost.***

18th May

It was this May Day in 1804 that Napoleon Bonaparte was finally declared Emperor of France by the French senate and a few months later the Pope gave Napoleon his blessing. Napoleon had actually been born in Italy ***and was known in France as - The Little Corsican.***

18th May

The man responsible for the only ever assassination of an English Prime Minister was executed today exactly one week after he pulled out a pistol and killed Spencer Percival. The killer died with his head in the noose ***and his skull was preserved at a Pathology museum.***

19th May

Born this May day in 1925 Nebraska USA was a boy named Malcolm Little but the world would know him by another name. He was the Muslim minister and human rights activist Malcolm X and both he and Martin Luther King ***were 39 at the time of their assassination.***

19th May

When Prince Harry wed Meghan Markle today in 2018 the occasion coincided with the anniversary of another Royal event. This was also the sunny day in May of 1536 that King Henry VIII's second wife Anne Boleyn became the ***first English Queen ever to be beheaded****.*

19th May

This very evening in 1962 all those watching were amazed when Blonde Bombshell Marilyn Monroe took to the stage and sang "Happy Birthday Mr President, Happy Birthday To You........" Sadly, this was one of ***the last performances Marilyn would ever give.***

20th May

The 'Legion of Honour' was established today in 1802 by Napoleon Bonaparte and is the highest French order of merit that can be awarded for civil and military recognition. This red ribboned medal of honour carries a motto ***which translates as 'Honour the Fatherland'****.*

20th May

Emilia Earhart boarded her plane today in 1927 taxied down the runway then took off from Newfoundland Canada landing in Ireland Ireland 24 hours later. This was the journey that saw amazing Amelia become ***the first woman to fly solo across the Atlantic.***

20th May

Published for the first time today in London 1609 by Thomas Thorpe were the Sonnet's written by William Shakespeare. The playwright had penned 54 sonnets and the most famous of these just has to be his wonderful ***Sonnet 18 - Shall I compare thee to a summer's day ?***

21st May

When Great Atlanta Fire of 1917 blazed away this day in May it left a path of destruction. Churches, business premises and almost 2,000 homes went up in smoke leaving 10,000 people homeless but the one fatality in the ***middle of this mayhem was caused by a heart-attack.***

21st May

It was this night in 1927 American aviator Charles Lindbergh in his Spirit of St. Louis monoplane completed the first ever non-stop solo Atlantic crossing. Flying from New York he landed in Paris where thousands of people were ***out on the streets in joyous celebration****.*

21st May

The Liverpool show was bouncing today in 1956 as thousands had gathered in Speke to join the fun in the sun. All eyes were on the skies as Daredevil Bird-man Leo Valentin leapt from an aeroplane to prove man could fly, but this ***was the moment Leo's life said goodbye.***

21st May

England's King Henry VI was murdered today in 1471 inside the Tower of London at the very midpoint of the Wars of the Roses and Richard of York it was who did the deadly deed. Henry was not much of a warrior King in fact ***- he was more of a writer than a fighter.***

22nd May

Born this day in 1946 was a boy who became a true Everton legend as a player and then later as manager. Who else but the late great Howard Kendall who along with Colin Harvey and Alan Ball formed a mighty midfield known ***by Goodison faithful as the 'Holy Trinity'****.*

22nd May

England's 'Wars of the Roses' lasted thirty long, bloody years and it all started today in 1455 at the Battle of St Albans. The 'Roses' refer to the Plantagenet Houses of Lancaster and York and these sworn enemies were in ***a bitter dispute for the Crown of England.***

22nd May

The Trevi Fountain was opened today in Rome 1762 and people just love to throw coins into this world famous fountain which collects a small fortune. To engage in the coin throwing you have to throw the coin ***right handed over your left shoulder and listen for the splash.***

23rd May

This sunny morning in 1934 two infamous American criminals in their getaway car were confronted by police in Louisiana. The couple had no way out as police opened fire pumping hundreds of bullets into their vehicle and ***the end of the ride was bloody for Bonnie & Clyde.***

23rd May

The Good Friday Agreement which had been signed 6 weeks earlier was accepted by the people of Northern Ireland today in 1998 in two referendums. Not everyone was in favour but the 75% that were meant it was ***a huge step forward in the quest to end The Troubles.***

23rd May

King Henry VIII finally got his marriage to Katherine of Aragon annulled today in 1533 almost 24 years after their wedding day. Henry had decided he should never have married his dead brother's wife after all and ***he had already secretly married Anne Boleyn.***

23rd May

Born today in London 1933 was Joan Collins who became one of the world's most famous. Her magnificent portrayal of Alexa in Dynasty sealed Joan's international superstardom and her knighthood from the Queen means it's ***true to say - There ain't nothing like a Dame.***

24th May

*After 14 years in the making Brooklyn suspension bridge was officially opened this sunny morning in 1883 by President Chester Arthur. This structure was built to withstand any weight and that included the giant parade of 21 Elephants **which would one day march across it.***

24th May

*British Battleship HMS Hood was attacked by Nazi Germany's The Bismarck today in 1941 and the Mighty Hood sank with the death of all but three on board. The Royal Navy immediately went after Bismarck with everything they had **and days later blew her to pieces**.*

24th May

*Born this sunny day in 1945 beneath the blue skies of NYC was a baby named Priscilla Ann Wagner and at a young age became besotted with Elvis Presley. Then at the age of 22 Priscilla married the man of her dreams and **for 6 years was Queen to the King of Rock n Roll.***

24th May

*The first Eurovision Song Contest was held today in Switzerland 1956 and 7 countries entered with the winning entry being a little number called Refrain by a lady named Lys Assla from the home nation and Eurovision is now **the longest running music show in the world.***

25th May

It was during the Falklands War this May day 1982 the HMS Coventry came under ferocious attack from the skies by Argentine aircraft causing ship to capsized with the loss of 19 lives. Remaining crew waiting to be rescued ***sang*** *-* ***Always look on the bright side of life.***

25th May

Two men thought it might be a good to steal an aeroplane so today in 2003 without being noticed the two climbed aboard a Boeing 727 and started the engine. They flew down the runway and went up, up and away but ***neither the men or the plane were ever seen again****.*

25th May

Richard Cromwell resigned from his role as Lord Protector of England today in 1659 after taking over from his dad Oliver eight months earlier. He had tried his best but Richard just couldn't fill his famous fathers boots and ***would be forever known as - Tumble down Dick****.*

25th May

Exactly one year on from the resignation of Richard Cromwell as Lord Protector and 4 days before he turned 30 Charles II landed at Dover today in 1660 at the invitation of the Convention Parliament. The Restoration period ***of the British Monarchy was about to begin.***

26th May

Marion Morrison was born today in 1907 USA and he grew up to become a movie star. The world knew him as the much admired John Wayne and it was written of him "Wayne is, of course marvellously indestructible ***and has become an almost perfect father figure".***

26th May

*The fifteen millionth 'Model-T Ford' rolled off the production line today in 1927 and became the last one ever made. This 20th century icon was affectionately known as the Tin-Lizzy and Henry Ford declared "****You can buy any colour you want as long as it's Black"****.*

26th May

One of the most famous novels in the world was first published today in 1897 and has since had many film and TV interpretations. Written by Bram Stoker this gothic horror story tells of a bloodthirsty Vampire living in ***Transylvania Romania as a Count named Dracula.***

27th May

San Francisco's world famous Golden Gate Bridge opened this sunny day in 1937 and boasted a span of 4,200 feet. During assembly there was a safety net between the bridge and the water 200 ft below and any worker who ***fell into the net joined the 'Halfway to Hell' club.***

27th May

The evacuation of WWII Allied soldiers from the beaches of Dunkirk which commenced today in 1940 took over a week to complete and was hailed a 'miracle of deliverance' by PM Winston Churchill. As this operation ***started on a Monday it was code named 'Dynamo'****.*

27th May

Launched today in 1967 by Jacqueline Kennedy in honour of her assassinated husband over 3 years earlier was the US Navy aircraft carrier USS John F Kennedy. Whilst Jackie was presiding over the launch ***her 9 year old daughter Caroline was at her side.***

28th May

The thundering roars of motorcycles shook the Isle of Man today in 1907 as the TT Races were ran for the first time. Riders compete for the Tourist Trophy in this event which is seen as one of the most dangerous racing events ***in the world and it even has 'Mad Sunday'****.*

28th May

Leonardo da Vinci's The Last Supper was very carefully put back on display today in 1999 Milan. This incredible work of art had just undergone a 22 year refurbishment and looks just as good today as it did when the ***great DaVinci finished it over 500 years ago.***

28th May

A boy named George was born today in 1660 and 54 years later he became Britain's King George I from the House of Hanover. It had taken this King over a month to arrive in England and claim his Crown and although he had a wife ***the woman by his side was his mistress.***

29th May

Hillary and Tenzing reached the very summit of the world's highest mountain today in 1953 and were the first mountaineers ever to do so making them national heroes. This giant mountain which stands over 29,000ft tall ***was named in honour of General George Everest.***

29th May

A pharmacist in Atlanta Georgia named John Pemberton placed an advert in The Atlanta Journal today in 1886 in an attempt to tempt people to buy a new drink he had made. This is now the second most consumed drink ***in the world after water and is called Coca-Cola.***

30th May

One day after the sinking of RMS Empress of Ireland with the loss of over 1,000 lives the ocean liner RMS Aquitania set sail from Liverpool today in 1914 on her maiden voyage and arrived at her New York destination ***6 days later with passengers and crew safe and sound.***

30th May

It was Pistols at Dawn this mild morning in 1806 with a dual between Charles Dickinson and Andrew Jackson in America. Dickinson fired first but his shot failed then Jackson fired and killed his opponent and a few years later ***Andrew Jackson became seventh US President.***

31st May

The largest Naval battle of World War I started today in 1916 as the British Grand Fleet engaged with the High Seas fleet of Germany. This Battle of Jutland raged until the following day and although the result was declared indecisive ***the British suffered the heaviest losses****.*

31st May

Many Roman Emperors had a tough time at the top. Some were executed others committed suicide and one unlucky soul was struck down by lightning and the Emperor known as Petronius Maximus was stoned to ***death today in 455 AD whilst trying to flee Rome****.*

June

From the Latin Junius and Juno the Roman Goddess of Marriage who was the Wife of the Supreme deity Jupiter

The Month of June is one of the 4 Months of the Year with Just 30 Days and is known for it's Sunshine

'Flaming June' is a late Nineteenth Century Work of Art by Frederic Leighton Housed in a Museum in Puerto Rico

They Say a Wedding in June is Good for the Bride and for the Groom and a Great Month for a Honeymoon

The Longest Day in the Northern Hemisphere and Shortest Day in the Southern Hemisphere Both Arrive in June

The Birthstone of June is the Pearl and the Two Zodiac Signs for this Month are Gemini and Cancer

No Month in any Year will Start on the Same Day as the Day that Starts the Month of June

The Full Moon of June is called the Strawberry Moon and This Beauty in the Sky Glows for Lovers Everywhere

That's a Fact !!

1st June

After being attacked by German fighter planes BOAC flight 777 from Portugal to the UK crashed into the Bay of Biscay today in 1943 killing all on board. Actor Leslie Howard was among the dead and it was later said ***the Germans believed Winston Churchill was on board.***

1st June

Germany's Adolf Eichmann was a major organiser of the Holocaust and after WWII he did a runner to Argentina where he assumed a different identity. But his past caught up with him and after being found guilty of his crimes ***this Nazi was executed today in 1962.***

2nd June

Ten months after taking office the 30th President of America Calvin Coolidge put pen to paper to paper this June day 1924 and signed the Indian Citizenship Act into law. This granted citizenship to all Native Americans ***born within the territorial limits of the United States****.*

2nd June

A stone-cold killer was born today in 1946 and his name was Peter Sutcliff the world knew him as the Yorkshire Ripper because Sutcliffe had murdered women in Yorkshire. Police needed a huge slice of luck to catch this killer and ***when they did he had murdered 13 women.***

3rd June

*King George V was born today in 1865 to Edward and Alexandra and when he ascended to throne at the age of 45 he was quite popular. This is the King who steered Britain through the Great War got rid of his German surname **and gave the first Royal radio broadcast.***

3rd June

*Two ships were taking part in military exercise Sea Spirit on this early June morning in 1969 when disaster struck. The Australian HMAS Melbourne and America's USS Frank E. Evans collided and the American ship **was literally cut in half resulting the loss of 74 lives**.*

4th June

*This sunny day in June 1896 Henry Ford completed what he called the Ford Quadricycle which was his first powered by petrol automobile. The success of this invention would lead to the founding of an Empire but for now **Henry just wanted to jump in and go for a spin**.*

4th June

*The ferocious Battle of Midway in the Pacific started today during WWII in 1942 and America claimed a decisive victory over Japan. This was just six months on from Pearl Harbour, emotions were running high and American forces **gave the Japanese the Whole Nine Yards.***

4th June

The Montgolfier brothers gave a demonstration of their first Hot Air Balloon today in France 1783 and onlookers watched in amazement. The tethered balloon was sent up and down several times but it remained empty ***as nobody would go up and down with it.***

5th June

In one of the most iconic images of the 20th Century a defiant lone student stopped Chinese military leaving Tiananmen Square today in 1989 by standing firm as they drove tanks towards him. It's not clear what happened to ***the student but he became known as Tank-Man.***

5th June

World champions England were playing Yugoslavia today in 1968 when Alan Mullery became the first English player ever to be sent off. Mullery had retaliated after being constantly fouled and was fined £50 but England manager ***Sir Alf Ramsay paid the fine for him.***

5th June

A young man appeared on the Milton Berle TV show this evening in 1956 to perform his new single. He started singing "You ain't nothing but a hound-dog........" and his suggestive hip movements left viewers feeling scandalised ***earning him the nickname 'Elvis the Pelvis'.***

5th June

Late this night in 1968 American Senator Robert Kennedy was addressing supporters in the Los Angeles Ambassador Hotel when an assassin shot him at close range. Hours later the Senator lay victim to a fatal bullet ***just as his older brother had done five years before.***

6th June

It was today in London 1844 the Young Men's Christian Association was founded with the aim of putting Christian principles into practise and creating a healthy body, mind and spirit in young men. Then 134 years later ***the YMCA went global with The Village People****.*

6th June

Robert Falcon Scott was born this sunny June day in 1868 and as he grew up he knew he wanted to explore the world. 'Scott of the Antarctic' he famously became known but although he and his men reached the South Pole ***their Terra Nova expedition proved fatal.***

6th June

Operation Overlord started today in 1944 when the Allies invaded Normandy to liberate France from the hands of the Nazis. This relentless assault was was driven by the combined forces of air, land and sea and ***this truly momentous day is remembered as D-Day.***

7th June

Henry VIII set up camp today in 1520 France with an army just outside Calais but his goal was not to fight the French or claim any land. Henry was throwing a giant banquet and the French King joined him in what ***became known as The field of the Cloth of Gold.***

7th June

England played Brazil today in the 1970 World Cup finals with the Brazilians winning 1-0. During this incredible game Pele thought he'd scored with a brilliant downward header only to see England keeper Gordon Banks make what ***became known as the Save of the Century***

7th June

The 'Yellow River Flood' was created this day in 1938 by the Chinese government in an effort to quell advancing Japanese forces in the second Sino-Japanese war. This caused the deaths of over 850,000 people and is the ***'largest act of environmental warfare in history'.***

7th June

Graceland in Memphis was home to Elvis Aaron Presley and thousands of his fans visit there every year to pay homage to the late great King of Rock n Roll. The house was first opened to the public today in 1982 but ***no-one was allowed into the bathroom of death****.*

8th June

A novel written by George Orwell was published today in 1949 one year after he wrote it. Then just 7 months after its publication the life of the author who's real name was Eric Blair came to an end and he would never ***see how meaningful Nineteen Eighty-Four would be.***

8th June

The untimely death of the Edward Prince of Wales this morning in 1376 was a shock to his father King Edward III and to England. The Prince had been a true warrior destroying the French at the Battle of Poitiers and ***history remembers him as Edward The Black Prince.***

8th June

There are many defining images from the twentieth century and one of them was captured today in 1972 during the Vietnam war. The heart-breaking image of a child badly burnt by napalm running for her life was ***captured on camera and shared for the world to see****.*

9th June

The Ghost Train has long been a must have ride at many amusement parks and there is always the occasional scream. But at the Luna Park in Sydney Australia today in 1979 the screams from the Ghost Train were for real ***as the ride burst into flames and killed 7 people.***

9th June

The most famous duck in the world made his debut today in 1934 and has been going strong ever since. Donald Fauntleroy Duck was the creation of Walt Disney and although he was a firm favourite he wasn't allowed ***into China because he didn't wear any pants.***

9th June

The ill-fated Julio-Claudian dynasty of Rome finally came to a bloody end today in 68 AD as evil Emperor Nero committed suicide before his own brutal guards could assassinate him. Nero was the Emperor who famously ***set fire to Rome and blamed it on the Christians.***

9th June

British wartime PM Winston Churchill had his first meeting with French President Charles De Gaulle this June day in 1940 to discuss their war effort. The burning question both men needed to find an answer to was ***- What are we going to do about Adolf Hitler ?***

10th June

BA flight 5390 was flying high in the sky today in 1990 when suddenly a cockpit windscreen exploded sucking the captain halfway through the windscreen. The plane diverted to Southampton with the captain hanging out of ***the window and amazingly the captain survived.***

10th June

Judy Garland who was born today in Minnesota USA 1922 was just a teenager when she played Dorothy in the Wizard of Oz and during filming the young actress would learn her lines, sing "Somewhere over the Rainbow" ***and smoke up to 200 cigarettes a day.***

10th June

Born this June day in 1921 was a boy named Philip Mountbatten who was awarded the Royal title Duke of Edinburgh as a wedding present when he married Princess Elizabeth 26 years. The Prince has had his occasional moments of ***calamity and once put a dint in a Hovercraft.***

10th June

Tally Ho and Off We Go......may have been the cry this afternoon on the River Thames London 1829 as the first ever Oxford v Cambridge boat race took place. Then 14 minutes 30 seconds later the crew that paddled the ***fastest and crossed the finish line first was Oxford.***

11th June

When a Mercedes-Benz collided with an Austin-Healey today in 1955 during the 24 Hours of Le Mans in 1955 outcome was catastrophic. Eighty three spectators were killed with another 100 injured and this remains ***the deadliest ever incident in the world of motorsport.***

11th June

King Henry VIII is well known for his 6 wives the first of whom was Katherine of Aragon and it was today in 1509 they tied the Royal knot. Henry was younger than his not so blushing bride who was also his sister-in-law ***having been married to his older brother Arthur****.*

11th June

There she was just a-walkin' down the street singin' Do wah diddy diddy dum diddy do. Snappin' her fingers and shufflin' her feet singin' Do wah diddy diddy……….. This instantly recognisable musical masterpiece was ***first recorded today in 1964 by Manfred Mann.***

11th June

King George II *ascended to the British throne today in 1727 following the death of his father George I. The new George was the second King from the House of Hanover, the last British Monarch born outside Britain and* ***the last British King to lead troops into Battle.***

12th June

Anne Frank was born this June day in Germany 1929 and as a teenager began writing her famous diary. Anne's father Otto had her diary published two years after her murder and it's believed Anne's older sister Margot ***also kept a diary but it has never been found****.*

12th June

When the movie premier of Cleopatra took place this evening in 1963 it starred Elizabeth Taylor and Richard Burton. The two famously became star-crossed lovers off set and although this wasn't the best movie in the world ***it was then the most expensive movie ever made.***

12th June

A powerful speech was delivered this day in June 1987 by fortieth American President Ronald Reagan at the Brandenburg gate. With the world watching he took one look at the 96 mile long structure before him and demanded ***"Mr Gorbachev Tear Down This Wall"****.*

12th June

A German born Jewish girl quietly celebrating her thirteenth birthday today in 1942 was given a diary as a present. Tragically the young girl would become a victim of the Holocaust but her now famous diary tells the tale of her time ***in hiding from the Nazis during WWII.***

13th June

A Royal Wedding took centre stage today in 1625 when King Charles I married his blushing Catholic bride Henrietta of France. Although their marriage seemed strong the King's grip on his crown was not and he would eventually ***pay the highest price for his weakness.***

13th June

In Dublin's fair city, Where the girls are so Pretty, I first set my eyes on sweet Mollie Malone, As she wheeled her Wheelbarrow through streets broad and......In Dublin 1699 a lady named Mary Malone died today and in 1988 ***this day was proclaimed - Mollie Malone Day****.*

13th June

The year was 1920 and for some time the US Post Office had been delivering babies for parents who posted their child to see their relatives. As long as the child weighed under 50 lbs then in the post they could go ***but today the US Post Office finally said No.***

13th June

The Queen was on her horse this sunny day in 1981 at the annual Trooping of the Colour celebrations in London when a young man fired six gun-shots towards her. The bullets turned out to be blank, the man was arrested and ***the startled Queen carried on Trooping.***

14th June

Born today in 1928 was Che Guevara and he became so famous his face ended up adorning millions of T-Shirts across the globe. Although he was well recognised as a Cuban revolutionist Che Guevara was born in Argentina ***and his real first name was Ernie****.*

14th June

The Peasant's Revolt had been raging for two weeks when Watt Tyler and his frenzied mob forced their way into the Tower of London today in 1831. Their target was Simon Sudbury who had introduced Poll Tax and when the ***peasants found Sudbury they chopped off his head.***

14th June

The fire that broke out and engulfed Grenfell Tower today in North London 2017 brought shock and horror to residents as 73 were killed in the blaze and many more injured. It quickly established the highly flammable ***exterior cladding was the major contributor to the terror***

14th June

The brutal Battle of Naseby took place today in 1645 during the English civil war and victory went to the Parliamentarians as Cromwell's new model army destroyed the Royalist forces. This battle was one of many in ***a war that lasted another six long years.***

15th June

This famous day in 1215 England's King John put his Royal seal of approval onto the Magna Carta in the fields of Runnymede down by the river Thames. Arguably the most famous gesture by an English King to his subjects ***since Canute tried to hold back the tide****.*

15th June

*A ship named the Terra-Nova set sail from Cardiff today in 1910 on an expedition of the same name and its destination was the frozen continent Antarctica. This became one of the most famous journeys made by man and **many a tale has been told of the men in the cold**.*

15th June

*The world's oldest Flag was adopted today in 1219 and it is the Red & White of Denmark. The story goes the Danes were doing battle when this flag fell from the sky and was caught by a Danish soldier their fortunes improved immediately **and the flag was adopted forever**.*

15th June

*A small plane landed in County Galway, Ireland today in 1919 and two men named John & Arthur climbed out. They had just completed the world's first none-stop transatlantic flight and their efforts were later rewarded **with a KBE and a £10,000 prize from the Daily Mail**.*

16th June

*After having a dabble a couple of years earlier it was today in USA 1903 Henry Ford launched his car company. His visionary thinking profoundly affected the future of the automobile industry and of all the cars he ever made **there are none more famous than Model-T.***

16th June

People have their favourite Hitchcock movie and one of those favourites was first shown on the big screen this evening in 1960. If you've seen the movie you'll remember the shower scene and if you haven't seen it you need to ***see it, a boy and his mum in PSYCHO.***

16th June

It was this June day 1967 a baby boy was born in Germany and as he grew up entered the world of professional football. Later joining the Premiere League he promised to bring Rock & Roll football to Anfield and that's exactly what he did - ***Happy Birthday Jürgen Klopp.***

16th June

Soviet cosmonaut Valentina Tereshkova was launched into orbit aboard Vostok 6 today in 1963 and made her very own piece of history as the first woman in Space. America needed a rocket up the backside if they ***were going to catch the Russians in the Space Race****.*

17th June

England's King Edward I was born today in 1239 and ascended to the throne aged 33 after keeping his own father locked in the Tower of London for more than seven years. Edward the warrior King reigned for 35 years and he ***became known as Hammer of the Scots.***

17th June

*Tonight in 1994 on the highways of L.A. a slow-speed getaway was unfolding as murder suspect O.J. Simpson was in the back of a truck being pursued by police and TV helicopters. Throughout his ordeal 'The Juice' held a gun to **his own head but he didn't pull the trigger.***

17th June

*Masked men broke into Washington DC HQ this evening in 1972 and subsequent investigations were monumental in American politics. This single act signalled the beginning of the end for President Richard Nixon as he became embroiled in the **Watergate Scandal.***

17th June

*A lady who arrived in New York Harbour today in 1885 was inside 214 crates and had a gigantic head with 7 spikes. Known as Lady Libertas after the Roman God of Freedom it took 4 months to put her together and this Lady now **stands proud as the iconic Statue of Liberty.***

18th June

*Another rallying speech from PM Winston Churchill today in 1940 which ended - Let us therefore brace ourselves to our duties and so bear ourselves, that if the British Empire and its Commonwealth last for a thousand years, **men will still say "This was their finest hour".***

18th June

Born in Liverpool today in 1942 was a boy who became a Beatle and one half of the world's most famous song writing duo. He and the three other band members changed the face of pop music forever so to Sir Paul McCartney ***of the Fab Four - Happy Birthday Macca****.*

18th June

When the Battle of Waterloo was fought today in 1815 it was almost 400 years on from the Battle of Agincourt. But Waterloo was fought and won on a Sunday and it was the last battle French Emperor Napoleon would ever fight ***as he abdicated 4 days after the fight****.*

19th June

Member of Parliament Sir Robert Peel was given the authority he had been waiting for from the House of Commons today in 1829 which allowed him to form the Metropolitan Police force. Soon after this the boys in blue became ***affectionately known as Bobbies and Peelers.***

19th June

Father's Day first fell on this Sunny Sunday in 1910 and the day is always celebrated on the third Sunday in June when fathers everywhere get nice new socks and possibly the odd tipple. Then nine months ***after Father's Day It's always Mothers Day.***

19th June

It was mare than 2 years after Abraham Lincoln's Emancipation Proclamation Declaration that Union troops arrived in Galveston Texas today and delivered the news that slavery was over. This monumental ***day in history is celebrated today as Juneteenth.***

19th June

Two highly controversial executions took place today in 1953 at Sing Sing Prison NYC when Julius and Ethel Rosenberg were Electrocuted for Espionage. Although they pleaded their innocence right up to the point of their death ***the law wouldn't listen to the Rosenbergs.***

20th June

Born this day in June 1949 was a boy who would grow up to be one of Motown's finest and his name is Lionel Richie. His debut single Truly set him apart from the rest and with Hello he got even better and Lionel is ***one of the best selling music artists of all time.***

20th June

When the life of King William IV ended today in 1837 he had reigned for just 6 years and was the oldest King ever to take to the throne. With no descendants the crown passed to his niece Victoria and her time at the top would ***last longer than any monarch before her.***

20th June

When must-see movie 'Jaws' was released today in 1975 audiences got a real bite-fright and the notes that accompany the approach of terror in the waters are now as well known as Beethoven's Fifth. The French labelled the film ***Les Dents De La Mer - The Teeth of the Sea****.*

20th June

Born this day in Tasmania 1909 was a boy who's personality, charm and chisel-chin good looks helped make him a Hollywood legend. He was the charismatic, swashbuckling Errol Flynn who said he had a fantastic life but ***didn't enjoy the two years he spent in London.***

21st June

Although Mussolini led one of the Axis powers during WWII he always seemed to be in the shadow of Adolf Hitler. Then today in 1940 the Italian leader decided the time was right to invade France but turns out the time ***was wrong and his invasion failed miserably.***

21st June

It was this June day in 1900 that an unhappy China formally declared war on Britain, the United States, Germany, France and Japan. They even turned on Chinese Christians who all fled to seek refuge with foreigners in what is ***famously known as the Boxer Rebellion****.*

21st June

Today is midsummer's day in the Northern Hemisphere and it is referred to as the longest day because there are more daylight hours than any other day in the year. This means we can all enjoy more hours of Sunshine ***today unless it happens to be cloudy.***

21st June

A masterclass display was deployed by Brazil today in Mexico 1970 as they beat Italy 4-1 in the World Cup final to lift the Jules Rimet trophy for the 3rd time. The defining moment in the game came when Carlos Alberto ***scored what was then hailed as the Goal of the Century.***

22nd June

The infamous World Cup 'Hand of God' took place this sunny afternoon in 1986 when Maradona pushed the ball into the net to score against England. He later scored a mesmerising goal to win the game for Argentina ***and both goals will always be remembered****.*

22nd June

The Coronation of George V took place today in 1911 just a year after his ascension to the British throne. To celebrate the occasion the all electric chimes of the Liver Bird clock rang out for the first time even though the ***Liver Building itself wasn't quite ready to move into.***

22nd June

When the World's first all electric Tower Clock was switched on this morning in 1911 high in the Liverpool sky the chimes that followed were in celebration of a King's Coronation. George V had ascended to the throne and today was his big day so it was time to chime.

22nd June

It was 7 months on from the start of the fall of the Berlin Wall and Berliners were travelling from East to West and back again. The iconic Brandenburg gate was open and it was this glorious sunny day in June that ***the infamous Checkpoint Charlie finally bit the dust****.*

23rd June

When Henry Hudson after whom the Hudson River is named wanted his ship to further explore Hudson Bay his crew refused and there was mutiny. Then today in 1611 Hudson, his son and 7 others were forced into a small boat ***by the mutineers and were never ever seen again.***

23rd June

The year was 1757 and three thousand British troops led by a man named Robert Clive were victorious today when they took on the might of a 50,000 strong Indian army. This victory consolidated British presence in Bengal and ***is known as the Battle of Plassey.***

23rd June

When the Battle of Bannockburn commenced this day in the Year 1314 Scottish forces led by Robert the Bruce easily defeated those of England's Edward II. The English King was a pale comparison to his famous father and this ***wasn't the only battle he would lose.***

24th June

Exactly 31 years after his Coronation the infamous King Henry VIII commanded his fourth wife Anne of Cleves to leave his court today. Anne was later declared Henry's 'beloved sister' given a nice house a generous income and ***lived a better life than the rest of his wives****.*

24th June

It was this sunny June morning in 1971 that the Wallasey tunnel known as Kingsway was opened by Her Majesty Queen Elizabeth II. More and more people now use the tunnels to commute whilst less and ***less people actually ever Ferry across the Mersey****.*

24th June

The Coronation of King Henry VIII took place today in 1509 four days before his 18th birthday and by his side was his wife Katherine of Aragon. Although the King would take 5 more wives his marriage to Katherine lasted ***longer than the rest of them put together.***

24th June

Nearly 500 American soldiers were captured and taken prisoner today in 1813 during the second War of Independence. They were attempting to make a surprise attack on British forces but were themselves ***attacked by American Indians and forced to surrender****.*

25th June

Born today in India 1903 a boy named Eric Arthur Blair who is better known as George Orwell the man who's novels include Animal Farm and Nineteen Eighty-Four. Within 250 yards of the house in which he called home ***in London there are now as many as 32 cctv cameras****.*

25th June

The Battle of Little Big Horn took place today in 1876 and General George Custer and his cavalry were annihilated by American Indians. Custer and his men were outnumbered, outfought and out-thought by the Indian braves in ***the Battle known as Custer's Last Stand.***

26th June

One King whose name always divides opinion is Richard III and he ascended to the throne today in 1483 after claiming his nephew Edward V was not the true heir. But Richard's reign would be short lived as ***he was slain at Bosworth just over two years later.***

26th June

When Elvis Presley performed before a sell-out crowd at the Madison Square Arena in Indianapolis this June evening 1977 the crowd loved every song he sang. Not one person present that evening had any notion this ***would become the night of the King's last ever concert*****.**

27th June

The bloody reign of Tudor Queen Mary I meant a terrible death for many Protestants as she attempted to force a return to Catholicism. Then in 1556 on this June day 11 men and 2 women known as the Stratford Martyrs ***were rounded up tied up then burned to death.***

27th June

Route 66 is one of the most famous highways in the world and journeying this long and winding road remains a dream for many and although this iconic highway was removed from the US highways system today in 1985 ***you can still go and get your kicks there.***

28th June

The Year was 1914 and Austrian Duke Franz Ferdinand decided to visit Sarajevo today even though he knew his life would be in serious danger. He still decided to make the fatal journey which cost him his life and his assassination ***led to the outbreak of WWI a month later.***

28th June

The signing of the Treaty of Versailles took place today in 1919 on the fifth anniversary of the assassination of Archduke Franz Ferdinand. The Japanese were very unhappy with the Treaty and such was the resentment ***in Germany it powered the rise of the Nazis Party.***

29th June

The USS Missouri was the place the Empire of Japan had surrendered ending WWII and America were proud of their battleship. Then today in 1989 in calmer waters pop star Cher filmed a raunchy video for her 'Turn Back Time' hit ***aboard the famous vessel and caused a storm.***

29th June

Blonde Bombshell, model and actress Jayne Mansfield was tragically killed in a car crash late this evening in 1967 after the car in which she was a passenger crashed into a lorry. The crash was so bad it was wrongly thought Jayne's head ***had been severed from her body.***

30th June

The world's first emergency telephone number was introduced this June afternoon in 1937 London following the deaths of 5 women in a house fire. The service was soon made available across the country and ***to make it easy for people to remember they chose 999.***

30th June

The Year was 1934 and although Adolf Hitler was now leader of the German nation the resistance he faced from some political rivals was starting to annoy him. Then on this night all those opposing his ways were ***systematically executed in the Night of the Long Knives****.*

July

The Seventh Month of the Year July was Named by the Roman Senate in Honour of their Great General Julius Caesar

This Month of 31 Days was once the Fifth Month of the Year and went by the Latin named of Quintilis

July symbolises the very Height of Summer in the Northern Hemisphere and the Middle of Winter Down Under

The God of July is the Mighty Jupiter who is God of the Sky and the King of All Gods in Roman Mythology

The Full Moon in July has Many Names including Buck Moon, Hay Moon, Rose Moon and Thunder Moon

The Birthstone for the Month of July is the Ruby symbolising Contentment and the Zodiac Signs are Cancer and Leo

There are a number of observances throughout July including World UFO Day, National Fried Chicken Day and Tiger Day

Crop Circles Appear in July and Crop Growers Everywhere say "Crops of Corn Should Be Knee High By the Fourth of July".

That's a Fact !!

1st July

Tragedy struck in the skies above Überlingen this night in 2002 when two planes collided killing everyone on board. A man who lost his entire family in the fatal crash was so devastated he tracked down the ATC he believed ***responsible for the collision and murdered him****.*

1st July

A clergyman of Protestant faith named John Bradford was executed this afternoon in 1558 on the orders of Bloody Mary. Like many of his associates before him Bradford was burned to death and it was he who coined the phrase ***– "There but for the grace of God go I".***

1st July

One of those must-have iconic inventions of the twentieth century was launched today in 1979 and millions of people flocked to buy their very own. This was a gadget like no other and was so popular over 200 million of them were sold ***the one and only Sony Walkman.***

2nd July

When people walking near Lake Constance looked to the skies above Germany today in 1900 they couldn't believe their eyes. What they were witnessing was the world's first flight of an airship and the man behind this flight ***of the future was Count Ferdinand von Zeppelin****.*

2nd July

*James A Garfield was the Twentieth President of the United States and had held office for just four months when he was fatally struck by an assassin's bullet today in 1881. Two months later Garfield's life was gone and **in stepped President number Twenty One.***

2nd July

*The world's most accomplished female aviator Amelia Earhart was flying with her co-pilot across the Pacific Ocean today in 1937 when they both disappeared. Despite the frantic searches that followed, Amelia her co-pilot **and her plane have never been seen again.***

3rd July

*The year was 1928 and a crowd gathered around a London hotspot to witness John Logic Baird switch on the world's first Colour TV. As the television set gradually became a corner stone in every home someone at the BBC **suggested people should pay for a TV licence**.*

3rd July

*Hard to believe the Earth is tens of thousands of miles further away from the Sun this July day than it is in January. Scientists always seem to have a name for anything that ever happens to this planet on which we live and **this phenomenon is known as Earth's Aphelion.***

3rd July

After seven hundred years away from its ancestral home it was announced today in 1996 by British PM John Major that the seat used for the Coronation of Scottish monarchs for many centuries 'The Stone of Scone' ***would finally and rightfully be retuned to Scotland.***

4th July

The FIFA World Cup final of 1954 became known as 'Miracle of Bern' after West Germany beat the Golden Team of Hungary 3-2 to lift the trophy today. The Germans wore a brand of boots that had been made made for the team ***by a Nazi called Adolf Dassler - Adidas.***

4th July

There are 50 stars on the American Flag and each star represents an American State. The 50th star was added to Old Glory on American Independence Day 1960 and it represents Hawaii the last State to join the Union ***and the only State positioned outside of North America****.*

4th July

When former American President John Adams breathed his last today in 1826 his last words were Jefferson lives but he was wrong because Thomas Jefferson had died hours earlier. Both men had signed the Declaration of Independence ***and both died on Independence Day.***

5th July.

A new company was founded today in 1994 and its founders knew it would change the way we shop forever. With their dynamic business model some revolutionary methods and a very good computer, they put the A-Z into ***online shopping and called the company Amazon****.*

5th July

In the Year 1948 a monumental decision made by a post-war government that would change healthcare in the UK forever. This was the day the National Health Service was founded in the UK and from ***that day to this we've been looked after by the NHS.***

5th July

Dolly the Sheep was born today in Scotland 1996 and became the first mammal ever to be cloned from an adult Somatic cell using the process the scientists call Nuclear Transfer. Dolly remains the world's most photographed ***sheep and she lived to the ripe old age of six****.*

6th July

It was late on this July evening in 1988 that terror struck Piper Alpha in the North Sea as a series of explosions ripped through the oil rig and destroyed her. This catastrophic disaster caused the deaths of 167 men ***and 30 of their bodies have never been recovered.***

6th July

Two young men from Liverpool met for the first time today in 1957 to discuss a future in the music industry. Their names were John and Paul and they formed an incredible song-writing partnership which made them ***famous across the globe as Lennon & McCartney****.*

6th July

Thomas More was one of Henry VIII's most trusted advisors but he pushed his luck too far and his head was chopped off this morning in 1535 on the orders of the King. Sir Thomas had objected to Henry's marriage to Anne Boleyn ***and that was a fatal mistake to make****.*

7th July

The youngest man to win a Wimbledon singles title did so today in 1985 and he was 17 year old German teenager Boris Becker. Each year in SW19 players smash balls with rackets, jump over the net, slip on the grass and umpires declare love, deuce and call for New balls.

7th July

The last of the people to face the death penalty for their part in the assassination of Abraham Lincoln went to meet their maker today in 1865 when they were all hanged. One of those facing the hangman became the ***first female to be executed by the US Government****.*

7th July

England's King Edward I was brutal, he banished Jews from England, fought a war against Scotland, executed William Wallace, had people hung drawn and quartered and often rode his luck and when died today ***it was on the 7th day of the 7th month in 1307.***

8th July

When the boys from Brazil faced Germany today in the semi-final of the 2014 World Cup both teams were unbeaten and a close result was expected but Germany didn't read that script. They destroyed the home nation 7-1 ***in a match described as national humiliation.***

8th July

In one last ditch attempt to avoid war with Great Britain the 'Olive Branch Petition' was signed today in 1775 and it beseeched King George III to avoid war with the 13 Colonies in America. But the King refused to even read it ***and labelled the colonists a bunch of traitors.***

8th July

The famous Liberty Bell rang out for the very first time today in Pennsylvania 1776 to announce the first public reading of America's Declaration of Independence. The bell has since been chipped so rings no more and It's ***Inscription which reads Pensylvania is spelt wrong.***

9th July

Johnny Weissmuller was one of the greatest swimmers of the 20th century who set over 50 world records and today in 1922 became the first person to swim the 100m freestyle event in under a minute. Once his record making ***days were over he simply turned into Tarzan.***

9th July

The twelfth President of the United States was Zachary Taylor and had only been in the job 16 months when his life ended unexpectedly today in 1850 following a short illness. Zachary is 1 of 4 presidents to ***die while holding office and the 2nd to die in the White House.***

9th July

One, two, three o'clock, four o'clock Rock, five, six, seven o'clock, eight o'clock Rock, nine, ten, eleven o'clock........... Bill Haley and his comets topped the billboard charts today in 1955 and Rock around the Clock became ***the first pop record to sell a million copies.***

10th July

It was 1985 and a vessel in New Zealand waters was attacked and sunk by two explosions. It seems the French were fed up with Greenpeace poking their nose into their affairs so they launched Opération Satanique ***and blew up the famous Rainbow Warrior****.*

10th July

When King Edward VI died today in 1553 his 1st cousin once removed became Queen de facto and all hell broke loose. Her name was Lady Jane Grey and she was quickly overthrown by Bloody Mary locked in the Tower of London ***and is remembered as the Nine Day Queen.***

10th July

There was once a statue of Britain's King George III in New York City but today in 1776 the Americans had seen just about enough of this King so tore the statue down and smashed it to pieces. America had declared their ***Independence from Britain and the King had to go.***

10th July

The Battle of Britain started today in 1940 and the Royal Air Force took to the skies to successfully defend the United Kingdom against the Nazi Luftwaffe in WWII. After more than three months the RAF were victorious and ***Germany failed in their Air battle for England.***

11th July

A famous duel took place this morning in 1804 in New Jersey as two American politicians faced each other for 'pistols at dawn'. Aaron Burr fired the shot that mortally wounded Alexander Hamilton and then he went back to ***his day job of being American Vice President.***

11th July

Published today in 1960 was the 281 page fictitious novel by Harper Lee which became a classic piece of American modern literature and a Pulitzer Prize winner. 'To Kill a Mockingbird' has been described as one of those books ***every adult should read before they die.***

11th July

A woman in Rome in 100 BC went into labour this evening and the next morning it was announced a baby boy had been born. The baby had a crooked nose and to the Romans that was a sure sign he would be a great leader ***and the name of this baby was Julius Ceasar****.*

11th July

King Henry VIII had again upset the Catholic Church and was excommunicated today in 1533 on the orders of the Pope but the English King didn't care in the least, he simply abolished Catholicism and then ***declared himself head of his new Church of England.***

12th July

An announcement in Rome this July morning in 100 BC was for the birth of a baby boy named Julius Ceasar who grew to become one of the world's great leaders. Spearheading the rise of the Roman Empire he was true to his word ***when he said - I came, I saw, I conquered.***

12th July

Henry VIII married his 6th wife Katherine Parr today in 1543 and she was a good match for him, this Queen managed to keep her head and even outlive her King. Henry is the most married English King and with 4 husbands ***Katherine is the most married English Queen.***

12th July

The Australian Aboriginal flag was flown for the first time today in 1971 on National Aborigines Day in Victoria Square Adelaide. This flag holds special status in Australia but it still took another 24 years for the ***Government to officially declare it a 'Flag of Australia'.***

12th July

Members of the Orange order will March today as they do every year to commemorate the victory for William III against deposed King James II at the Battle of Boyne in 1690. The two men were actually in-laws as ***William was married to James's eldest daughter Mary.***

13th July

Ruth Ellis became the last woman ever to be hanged in the United Kingdom this day in 1955 after pleading guilty to the murder of her abusive lover. Ruth's execution took place in Holloway prison and her hangman was ***a Yorkshireman named Albert Pierrepoint.***

13th July

It was during the of English civil war the Battle of Roundway Down took place this day and victory went to the Royalists. The king's men were jubilant after their victory but celebrations would all be short-lived in this war ***as there was a lot more blood still to spill.***

13th July

Today celebrates another anniversary of Live Aid at Wembley in 1985 when musicians put on a concert raising money to help fight starvation and suffering in Ethiopia. Rockers Status Quo opened the show and the first track ***performed was - Rocking all over the World.***

13th July

A boy named Erno was born this July day in Budapest Hungary 1944 and became known to the world as Dr. Erno Rubik inventor of the Rubik's Cube. Such was the phenomenal success of the Cube today is celebrated annually as ***International Puzzle Day in honour of Erno.***

14th July

When the first ascent of the Matterhorn was made today in 1865 the successful climb was quickly followed by tragedy when 4 of the party fell to their death. One climber slipped and pulled 3 others with him and what followed ***after this were false allegations of rope-cutting****.*

14th July

When Wild West gunfighter Billy the Kid was shot and killed this day in 1881 by sheriff Pat Garrett rumours started circulating his death was a hoax. The Kid was just 21 years old but such was his fame that more than fifty people ***later claimed to be the real Billy the Kid.***

14th July

Bastille Day is celebrated today each year in France to remember the storming of the Bastille prison in 1789 which was a turning point of the French Revolution. It took the French a while to make this their National Day but ***they do celebrate it rather well - 'Vive la France'****.*

15th July

The Peasants Revolt of 1381 was a challenging time for the young King Richard II but he had quelled the riot and taken his revenge. Then this afternoon he watched with satisfaction as conspirator and trouble maker ***John Ball was Hanged, Drawn and Quartered****.*

15th July

10 Rillington Place was the address of serial killer John Reginald Christie who was finally hanged for his evil crimes today in 1953. Claiming to be medically trained he would lure unsuspecting women to his home for a cure ***but they were never seen alive again****.*

15th July

Born today in Manchester 1858 was a baby girl who grew to become one of those people never to be forgotten. This Suffragette leader fought all the odds to get women their deserved right to vote, she left an enduring ***legacy and her name is Emmmeline Pankhurst.***

15th July

The July revolt of 1927 started in Vienna when protestors took to the streets today and the terror that followed left 600 police injured and a similar number of protestors also injured. Worse still there were 5 policemen and ***89 protesters killed in this July 15th Massacre.***

16th July

The Coronation of an English King took place this July day in 1377 as 10 year old Richard II was crowned at Westminster Abbey. The young King had ascended to the throne following the death Edward III and had a ***misplaced belief that God was always on his side****.*

16th July

Uruguay won their second World Cup this day in 1950 beating Brazil in front of a record crowd to lift the Jules Rimet trophy. The winning goal-scorer that day went on to outlive everyone on the pitch and actually died on the ***65th anniversary of his World Cup winning goal****.*

16th July

*JFK said America would be the First Nation to put man on the moon. Then today in 1969 it was lift-off from Kennedy Space Station for Apollo 11 and four days later man landed on the moon just as JFK had promised but **the President hadn't lived long enough to see it.***

16th July

*Authorised by President Harry S.Truman, the first detonation of an atomic bomb took place today in 1945 in the State of New Mexico. America were testing the power and ferocity of their latest weapon of war in a secret **operation codenamed the Manhattan Project.***

17th July

*The Hundred Years War between England and France finally reached its conclusion today in 1453 at the bloody Battle of Castillon. It was the French who seized the initiative on the battlefield and were so swift and decisive the **English were overwhelmed and destroyed.***

17th July

*The fate of RMS Carpathia was sealed this afternoon in 1918 after she was torpedoed by a German U-boat and went to her watery grave. This was the wonder-ship that came to the aid of RMS Titanic and plucked survivors **from the Atlantic Ocean six years earlier.***

17th July

The very first Disneyland there park opened this sunny morning in 1955 California complete with the iconic Sleeping Beauty Castle and the people just poured in. This is Disney's only theme park that was designed and ***built under the supervision of Walt Disney himself****.*

17th July

When the Hundred Years war between England and France finally reached its inevitable conclusion today in 1453 it had actually lasted 116 years. The overwhelming French victory meant that England had now lost every stronghold in France ***apart from the port of Calais.***

18th July

Over 200,000 people turned out this warm sunny day in 1934 to witness King George V officially open Queensway Tunnel connecting Liverpool with Birkenhead. The tunnel's completion had taken nine years and when opened ***was the longest road tunnel in the world.***

18th July

The Olympic Games were taking place today in Montreal 1976 when judges and the world saw what they had never seen before. A 14 year old girl named Nadia Comaneci did her routine on the uneven bars and became ***the first gymnast in the world to score a Perfect 10.***

18th July

*An Austrian who dreamt of becoming a German citizen and fought for Germany in WWI had been locked in prison where he managed to write a book. This book was published today in 1925 the author was Adolf Hitler and he gave **his book the title Mein Kampf.***

18th July

*When King Edward I ordered the expulsion of all Jews from England this day in 1290 all monies owed to Jewish money lenders became payable to the Crown. It was 350 years later that Jews were allowed to return but they **had to pay Oliver Cromwell for the privilege.***

19th July

*The Mary Rose was Henry VIII's most famous ship but she was sunk today in 1545 during battle with the French in the straits of the river Solent. The Tudor King was standing on the Portsmouth dock and watched in disbelief as **his beloved ship sank before his very eyes**.*

19th July

*The Great Fire of Rome started today in 64 AD and raged for six days and five nights destroying half the city. It's believed Emperor Nero started the blaze then blamed it on the Christians but perhaps the Christians responded **"We didn't start the fire – Nero is a Liar".***

19th July

A controversial attack on the city of Rome took place today in 1943 by Allied forces during WWII. The Eternal City was hit by over 1,100 tons of bombs from 500 American bombers and Churchill agreed with this act but ***people across the world said "Leave Rome alone".***

19th July

The world famous Royal Liver Building opened for business this July morning in 1911 and is one of the Three Graces on the Liverpool waterfront. Two mythical Liver Birds Bella & Bertie stand atop this iconic structure and ***its clock face is bigger than the face of Big Ben****.*

20th July

An assassination attempt made on Adolf Hitler this afternoon in 1944 by one of his own Colonels failed to kill the Fuhrer and that was bad news for many. The would be assassin was soon arrested, severely tortured, ***then executed and so were his family and friends****.*

20th July

Happy Birthday to Roger Hunt who was born today in 1938. Sir Roger wore the famous number 7 shirt, scored when Liverpool won their first FA Cup, holds the record for the most league goals scored for the club and is the ***only Red with a World Cup winners medal.***

20th July

This was a dark day for London's Regent and Hyde Parks in 1982 when bombs planted by the IRA exploded in each location. Eight soldiers and seven horses were killed in the blast and another 100 people were injured ***on what should have a quiet summers day.***

20th July

America's Central Intelligence Agency who's unofficial motto reads 'And ye shall know the truth and the truth shall make you free'. Had to come clean today in 1977 under the Freedom of Information Act admitting ***they were heavily involved in mind-control experiments.***

21st July

England's King Henry IV had usurped the throne from Richard II with ease and then today in 1403 had to fight to keep his crown. The King defeated rebel forces at the Battle of Shrewsbury which saw English archers fight ***English archers on English soil for the first time****.*

21st July

While Neil Armstrong and Buzz Aldrin were enjoying walking on the Moon today in 1969 the third astronaut Michael Collins had to stay in the space module and wait for them. It has since become known that Neil and Buzz were American born ***while MIchael was born in Italy.***

21st July

"That's one small step for a man, one giant leap for mankind" said Neil Armstrong today in 1969 when he stepped onto the surface of the Moon later to be joined by Buzz Aldrin. ***So after waiting billions of years for a man to walk on the moon two turned up at once.***

21st July

Gun-fighter Davis Tutt more than met his match today in 1865 when he took on Wild Bill Hickok in what is regarded as the first gun-fight of the Wild West. Tutt found out the hard way that if you're gonna ***live by the gun then you're gonna die by the gun.***

22nd July

Prince William and Kate celebrated the birth of the first child today in 2012 and from all the names they had to choose from they chose George. What they didn't know then was they would soon have another son and ***that son would be born on Saint George's Day.***

22nd July

American gangster and bank robber John Dillinger was shot and killed by Chicago police this very evening in 1934 while making his escape from a local theatre. Dillinger had robbed 24 banks and holds the dubious honour ***of being the FBI's first ever Public Enemy No1.***

22nd July

It was during the Scottish Wars of Independence that the Battle of Falkirk was fought today in 1297 with King Edward I destroying the forces of William Wallace. Victory tasted sweet for Longshanks and it was thanks ***mainly to the arrows of his Longbow men.***

22nd July

The Norway Attacks took place today in 2011 and were carried out by one individual. It began with a bomb blast that killed 8 and injured 209 more before the armed killer made his way to a youth camp and fired indiscriminately ***killing 69 people and injuring another 110.***

23rd July

Born this July day in London 1965 was a boy named Saul Hudson who was destined to become one of the world's greatest guitar players as part of rock band Guns N' Roses. He decided he wanted a real Rock n Roll name and ***there was one that stood out from the rest - 'Slash'.***

23rd July

A baby girl born today in 1973 USA made headline news 25 years later after President Bill Clinton referred to her as 'that woman'. And in the blink of an eye Monica Lewinski became famous across the globe as did her ***nice blue dress which she had bought from Gap****.*

23rd July

"Help, I need somebody, Help, not just anybody, Help, you know I need someone"............... Another Lennon & McCartney masterpiece released today in 1965 and another chart topper for the Fab-Four as well as the theme song to ***their new movie of the same name****.*

24th July

The year was 1704 and the War of Spanish succession was in full throttle with many fighting gallantly for the throne of Spain. While all the commotion was going on Britain decided to make their own move today and captured ***a piece of Spanish rock named Gibraltar.***

24th July

Things were getting hot under the collar today in 1974 for President Richard Nixon when the United States Supreme Court ruled he had no authority to hold onto White House tapes and ordered him to release them. ***This was another nail in the coffin of the Watergate scandal.***

24th July

'At the third stroke the time will be 9 O'Clock precisely' Ethel Jane Cane first spoke these words on the telephone this morning in 1936. Ethel had won a competition to be the first person to tell the time on the telephone and was ***known as 'The girl with the golden voice'.***

25th July

This afternoon in the year 2000 Air France flight No 4590 was set ablaze after striking a metal object on the runway during takeoff from Charles de Gaulle Airport. The resulting crash and tragic loss of life signalled the ***beginning of the end for the majestic Concorde.***

25th July

The derailment of a train in Spain today in 2013 which caused the deaths of 79 people and injured 140 more was caused by the train travelling twice as fast as it should have been. The driver was later charged with ***79 counts of homicide by professional recklessness.***

25th July

A healthy baby girl was born this July day in Oldham 1978 and the world's media had been watching and waiting for the arrival of this bundle of joy. But this was no ordinary baby event, this was the birth of Louise Brown and ***she was the world's first test tube baby.***

26th July

Argentina went into mourning today in 1952 following the untimely death of Eva Perón wife of the country's President. This First Lady known as Evita was just 33yrs old and had fought for the millions of people during her lifetime ***but she just couldn't fight the Cancer.***

26th July

After guiding the country to VE Day in WWII Winston Churchill resigned from office today in 1945 "I've been given the Order of the Boot" he quipped. This meant the great leader wasn't PM when the war started ***and wasn't PM when the war ended either****.*

26th July

The thirteenth release of a Walt Disney animated movie took place this afternoon in London 1951 and the movie was Lewis Carroll's Alice in Wonderland. Although given the thumbs down by film critics at the time the movie ***has since become an animated cult classic.***

26th July

Founded this July day in 1908 by American President Theodore Roosevelt and John Edgar Hoover was the 'Federal Bureau of Investigators'. Known as the FBI this unique organisation is now quite possibly the ***most famous law enforcement agency in the world.***

27th July

It was during the reign of King William III and his wife Queen Mary that the Bank of England was founded today in 1694 and was set up as the Government's Bank. Located in central London it is now affectionately known as ***the Old Lady of Threadneedle Street.***

27th July

*The King Charles I Cavaliers faced Cromwell's Roundheads this July day in 1642 at the Battle of Gainsborough during the English Civil War. Victory was swift for Cromwell's men but this war still had another nine years to run **before it reached its bloody conclusion**.*

27th July

*The deadliest single Cannon shot in history was fired today in 1816 from a US Gunboat and it's point of impact was the enemy's own gunpowder store. The resulting explosion was so powerful it ripped through their fort **killing 275 people and that was game over.***

27th July

*It's full title is the : Convention relative to the Treatment of Prisoners of War , Geneva July 27, 1929 but is known as the Geneva Convention and it was today this historic declaration was agreed. Unfortunately the terms of the **agreement were ignored by many during WWII**.*

28th July

*It was 1945 and a small plane flying in dense fog above New York City crashed into the Empire State Building killing pilot and passenger. In the melee that followed the lift dropped over 75 floors but the lady Inside the lift named Pat **miraculously survived the high speed drop**.*

28th July

After being trapped deep underground for 77 hours in the Quecreek mine in Pennsylvania in 2002 the end was in sight today for 9 tired miners desperate to get back above ground. All men were safely rescued from the mine but they were freezing cold and looked purple.

28th July

The wedding of King Henry VIII and Fifth wife Catherine Howard took place today in 1540 and Henry seemed very happy with his young bride at his side. While the wedding ceremony was taking place the King's key advisor ***Thomas Cromwell was being executed for treason***

29th July

Vincent Van Gogh had held a pistol to his chest and pulled the trigger and today in 1890 was his last. The flawed genius had sold just one painting in his lifetime and never knew how valuable his work would become, his 'Starry Night' ***even inspired a No1 song in the 1970's.***

29th July

When Prince Charles married Lady Diana Spencer today in 1981 a worldwide TV audience watched as the newly weds walked down the aisle, exchanged vows and then kissed on the balcony. Although dubbed the 'wedding of the century' ***their marriage was doomed.***

29th July

*After the 12 year hiatus the Summer Olympic Games started today in London and 59 countries took part. The Germans and Japanese were not invited and the Russians stayed at home one of the stars of the games was **Fanny Blankers-Koen aka 'The Flying Housewife'.***

30th July

*This was 1966 and England won the World Cup beating West Germany 4-2 after extra time in the final at Wembley. Geoff Hurst scored the only ever World Cup Final hat-trick and the Jules Rimet trophy was presented **to Bobby Moore by her majesty the Queen**.*

30th July

*An act of sabotage took place today in New York Harbour 1916 when German agents blew up US munitions during WWI. Over $20,000,000 worth of military goods were destroyed with 4 people killed in what is one of the **largest man-made non-nuclear explosions in history**.*

30th July

*The final showing of Tops of the Pops took place this July evening in 2006 after the BBC caved in and called it quits on the show that had brought music to the nation for over 42 years. The last performance on the show was by **Shakira with her No1 song - Hips don't Lie.***

31st July

Born this day in 1965 in Gloucestershire was a girl who became the great novelist, philanthropist, movie producer, screenwriter and creator of Harry Potter. Her name is J.K.Rowling and she decided to give her very own ***wonderful wizard the same birthday as herself.***

31st July

The British Armed Forces 'Operation Banner' during The Troubles in Northern Ireland finally ended today in 2007 after almost 38 years. Their role was to support the Royal Ulster Constabulary in what was the longest ***continuous deployment in British military history****.*

31st July

Born this day in 1965 in Gloucestershire was a girl who became the great novelist, philanthropist, movie producer, screenwriter and creator of Harry Potter. Her name of course is J.K. Rowling and she decided to ***give her Wonderful Wizard the same birthday as herself****.*

August

This Eighth Month of the Year once had Just 29 Days and is Named in Honour of Roman Emperor Augustus

It is said Augustus added Two Days to this Month that bore his Name as He didn't want Less Days than Caesar's July

August originally went by the Latin name Sextilis as it was the Sixth Month of the Year in the 10 Month Calendar

North American Fishing communities called the August Moon the Sturgeon Moon as this Fish Fills their Lakes this Month

In the Southern Hemisphere August is Cold and Wet whilst in The Northern Hemisphere it's Time for Hot, Sunny Holidays

The Birthstone for the Month of August is the Peridot and the Two Signs of the Zodiac are Leo and Virgo

August is a Very Popular Boys Name in Sweden with many of these Boys being Born in the Month that shares their Name

Alphabetically speaking August Follows April and is one of Five Months of the Year that has 744 Hours

That's a Fact !!

1st August

MTV was launched this August morning 1981 with the words "Ladies and Gentlemen, rock and roll" and the first music video to greet those watching was "Video Killed the Radio Star" and the channel proudly announced ***"You'll never look at music the same way again".***

1st August

Following the passing of Queen Anne today in 1714 the reign of the House of Stuart came to an end in Britain today after 7 monarchs had ruled for just over 111 years between them. This particular dynasty was not the best ***for Britain and some reigns were catastrophic.***

2nd August

Wild Bill Hickok was playing poker this afternoon in 1876 at the Number Ten saloon in South Dakota when he was shot in the back and killed. The gunfighter slumped to the floor holding Aces & Eights in Clubs & Spades ***4 cards now known as the Dead Mans Hand****.*

2nd August

Jewish prisoners at Treblinka death camp in Poland staged a revolt against their Nazi captors today in 1943 but sadly they faced near-total slaughter. Only around 70 of them managed to escape from this place of death where ***as many as 900,000 Jews had been murdered.***

3rd August

After a year in the making the world's first themed amusement park opened its doors today in 1946 to the delight of many in Santa Claus Indiana. The name has changed but the park is still going strong with over 1,000,000 ***thrill-seekers each year going along for the ride.***

3rd August

The first American intercollegiate sporting event took place today in 1852 as Harvard University beat Yale University in the Boat Race. Harvard is named after Englishman John Harvard who bequeathed half of his estate to them and ***Harvard will remember John forever.***

4th August

The Battle of the Solent took place today in 1588 and the forces of Queen Elizabeth I held off the Spanish Armada stopping Spain from seizing the Isle of White. Elizabeth's forces eventually prevailed over the Spanish and ***the Queen gave thanks to her forces and to God****.*

4th August

Following a tip-off from a Dutch informer this August day in 1944 German Gestapo raided an Amsterdam building. Forcing their way into a sealed off area they found and arrested diarist Anne Frank and her family and ***for these Jewish people it was the start of the horror.***

4th August

England's Edward III was handed the keys to Calais today in 1347 ending an eleven month siege that had tested his patience to the limit. Six men known as the Burghers of Calais feared for their lives as they faced the King ***but Edward decided to let them live.***

5th August

Born today in 1930 was a boy who became fascinated with outer space and grew up wanting to become an astronaut. He had no idea how famous he would become as the first man ever to walk on the surface of ***the moon and his name was Neil Armstrong.***

5th August

The fortieth President of America Ronald Reagan was seen as Mr. Nice Guy by many and Mr. Mean by many others. During his time in office 11,359 air-traffic controllers went on strike and ignored his order to return to work ***so today in 1984 he fired every one of them.***

5th August

The life of a true Hollywood Icon sadly ended this morning in 1962 as the lifeless body of Marilyn Monroe was found at her California home seemingly the victim of a drugs overdose. Some years later Elton John sang that Norma Jean ***had lived her life like a Candle in the Wind.***

6th August

*The first woman to successfully swim the English Channel did so this day in 1926 and her name was Gertrude Ederle. Swimming from France to England it was Gertrude's second attempt but her time of just over eleven hours **was almost twice as fast as the first man.***

6th August

*It was at Auburn prison in New York 1890 on this August day that convicted murderer William Kemmler became the first man executed by Electric Chair. An audience was selected to watch the killer die but all did not go to plan **and this became a very gruesome execution.***

6th August

*In an attempt to force Japan to surrender in WWII it was this sunny August in 1945 America dropped the Atom bomb on Hiroshima. Little Boy was the name of the bomb that caused so much horror and the plane that dropped it **was named after the pilot's mother Enola Gay.***

7th August

*Californian Superior Court Judge Harold Haley was taken hostage by gunmen and murdered today in 1970 whilst presiding over a trial in his own courtroom. The criminals from San Quentin bundled the Judge into a van **then shot him at close range in the face and chest.***

7th August

In the early hours of this morning in 1985 a family were slaughtered in their beds and the investigating DCI immediately accepted this was murder-suicide. It was only thanks to one determined policeman who would not give up that the ***'White House Murders' killer was caught.***

7th August

Shakespeare's most famous tragedy is quite possibly the story of Macbeth and it is believed the play was first performed today in 1606 for Stuart King James I. In the world of theatre many people believe Macbeth is cursed and only ***refer to this work as 'The Scottish Play'****.*

7th August

French daredevil Phillipe Petit performed a death-defying high-wire act this morning in 1974 between the Twin Towers of the World Trade Centre in New York City. The streets of Manhattan came to a standstill as ***everyone stared in amazement at this Man on a Wire****.*

8th August

It was in the early hours of this morning in 1963 the 'Great Train Robbery' took place at Bridego bridge in Buckinghamshire and the plucky robbers got away with £2.6m in cold hard cash. The day also just happened ***to be the 34th birthday of a certain Ronnie Biggs.***

8th August

The Fab Four were photographed walking across a zebra crossing today in 1969 and the iconic image became the cover of the album Abbey Road. John leads the way followed by Ringo, Paul then George and this is their only album ***without the Beatles name on the cover.***

8th August

Less than 2 months after his defeat at Waterloo Napoleon Bonaparte boarded a ship today in 1815 bound for St Helena where he'd live out his days. The British demanded the former Emperor be exiled and this baron South Atlantic ***Island was 1,200 miles from anywhere****.*

8th August

In 1907 the world's first ever Boy Scouts camp was coming to an end today near Poole in Dorset. Lord Baden Powell had taught the boys to live by the scouting code, play games, cook beans on the camp fire, and joyfully ***sing their favourite song****.........* ***'Ging Gang Goolie'****.*

9th August

The Leaning Tower of Pisa is one of the most instantly recognisable structures in the world. Construction of this unique tower started this August day in 1173 and although it took them over 200 years to build the tower the Italians ***still couldn't manage to get it straight****.*

9th August

The Coronation of King Edward VII took place at Westminster Abbey today in 1902 and by his side was Queen Alexandra. The ceremony was scheduled to take place 7 weeks earlier but appendicitis meant celebrations had been ***on hold until the King was back to his best****.*

9th August

The Japanese city of Nagasaki faced the horror of the Atomic bomb today in 1945 three days after the same bombing of Hiroshima. With agreement from the UK, American President Harry S Truman ordered the mass destruction after ***having held office for just four months.***

9th August

Richard Nixon became the only President ever to resign from office when he did so today in 1974 following the now infamous Watergate Scandal. The investigation that shocked a nation had Nixon famously declaring ***"There'll be no Whitewash at the White House".***

10th August

Born today in 1874 was Herbert Hoover and he became America's 31st President. Hoover couldn't recover the crash of '29 but he was the first man to switch on the lights to the Empire State Building and he ***does have a Dam in Nevada named in his honour****.*

10th August

The unfortunate King Louis XVI of France was arrested today in 1792 after his palace was stormed by a Parisian mob during the French Revolution. His own Swiss Guards were massacred during the siege and the future for ***this French King wasn't looking too good either****.*

10th August

News of America's Declaration of Independence reached King George III this August morning in 1776 over a month after it had been declared. Two bloody wars would follow Britain would lose them both and George III ***would be labelled - The Last King of America.***

10th August

The 'Treaty of London of 1641' was signed this August day which put an end to the Bishop's Wars between England and Scotland. The wars had been caused when Stuart King Charles I attempted to impose a new prayer book ***which created patriotic and religious outrage.***

11th August

The first ascent of the Eiger took place today in 1858 when 3 men reached the summit after climbing the west flank to get there. The Eiger reaches 13,015 ft into the sky and has the most treacherous north face in the Alps ***where many climbers have tried and died.***

11th August

Ronald Reagan gave the American nation quite a shock this August day in 1984 during his quest for re-election to the White House. While preparing his weekly address to the nation on National Public Radio the President ***quipped "We begin bombing in five minutes"****.*

11th August

Alcatraz Federal Penitentiary opened this sunny August morning in 1934 on the rock of San Francisco Bay and this supposedly escape-proof prison was home to the criminally insane. Alcatraz held many notorious inmates ***including infamous Chicago mobster Al Capone.***

11th August

The 'Mall of America' enjoyed it's grand opening the sunny August morning in Minnesota 1992 and thousands turned out to join in the fun. The monster Mall boasts 520 stores and if you ever wondered why they call it a Mall ***it's because you can go in and shop them-all.***

12th August

Disaster struck Japanese Airlines Flight 123 today in 1985 when the aircraft crashed into a mountainside killing 520 people. Pilots had lost control but tragedy was caused by faulty repair work to the plane and is the ***deadliest single-aircraft disaster in the history of aviation.***

12th August

The fascinating life of beautiful Egyptian Queen Cleopatra came to an end this very evening in 30 BC. Overwhelmed with sorrow following the suicide of her lover Mark Anthony the mourning Queen took an Asp held it to ***her chest then succumbed to it's poisonous bite.***

12th August

Each year in Great Britain the Grouse Shooting season starts today and can last for almost two months. The season can start on any day of the week but never on a Sunday and no matter what day it starts this August day is ***famously known as the 'Glorious Twelfth'****.*

12th August

The horrific week long series of mass murders in Poland came to an end today in 1944 during WWII after Nazis had systematically murdered tens of thousands of Poles including women, children and babies. This time of ***terror is remembered as the Wola Massacre****.*

13th August

Following their historic journey to the Moon and back the Astronauts of Apollo 11 received a ticker-tape parade through packed streets of NYC today in 1969 and later enjoyed a state dinner in LA where they were awarded ***Presidential Medal of Freedom by Richard Nixon****.*

13th August

In a precise military operation this August night 1961 the Berlin Wall separating East from West Germany was laid from the first brick to the last. By morning no-one was allowed to cross through this 96 mile long wall of death ***and it stayed that way for the next 28 years****.*

13th August

Born this August day in London 1899 was Sir Alfred Joseph Hitchcock and he became one of the most influential filmmakers in the history of cinema. It seems all movie-buffs all have their favourite Hitchcock movie and ***Alfred's very own favourite was - Shadow of Doubt.***

13th *August*

Gwynne Evans and Peter Allen were executed this morning in 1964 having been found guilty of murdering a man named John West. Both were hanged simultaneously in Manchester Strangeways and Liverpool Walton ***making them the last men hanged in Britain.***

14th August

A recorded speech by Emperor Hirohito played to the Japanese nation today in 1945 announcing the end of WWII hostilities caused mass confusion. This was the first time the people had heard the Emperor's voice and ***most could not understand what he was saying****.*

14th August

Operation Banner started today in 1969 when British Armed Forces appeared on the streets of Northern Ireland as part of The Troubles to keep the peace. What followed was anything but peaceful and the 35 year deployment ***is the longest in British military history.***

14th August

Cathedral fever descended on Germany today in 1880 particularly in the city of Cologne as it became a national day of celebration across the land. After 632 years the country's largest Cathedral was opened and this magnificent structure ***houses the Shrine of the Three Kings****.*

14th August

Liverpool's very own Sir Paul McCartney performed a sell-out concert this August night in 2014 at San Francisco's famous Candlestick Park. The site was due to be demolished so who better than a former Beatle to give ***the iconic stadium the send off it deserved.***

15th August

Napoleon Bonaparte was born this August day in Corsica 1769 and at the time Corsica belonged to Italy so Napoleon grew up resenting the French long before he became their greatest Emperor. Well you know what they say ***"If you can't beat them join them".***

15th August

The Mongol Empire was a supreme fighting force who could never conquer Japan. Kublai Khan tried today in 1281 with 4,000 ships and 140,000 men but Mother Nature pulverised his fleet with a typhoon of terror that ***the Japanese called the Divine Wind or 'Kamikaze'.***

15th August

The Panama Canal joining the Atlantic and Pacific Oceans opened for business today in 1914 but this wonder of the modern world came at a high cost. The 51 mile route took over 30 years to complete and during construction ***the mortality rate ran to thousands of men.***

15th August

During their 1965 American tour the Fab Four played a concert this August evening at the Shea Stadium in New York City to a crowd of almost 60,000 screaming fans. Such was the success of the concert that ***this single event is regarded as the birth of 'Stadium Rock'.***

16th August

When the life of music legend Aretha Franklyn came to an untimely end today in 2018 it was exactly 41 years after the untimely death of music legend Elvis Presley. Ironic that this August day would became the last for ***the Queen of Soul and for the King of Rock'n'Roll.***

16th August

The most violent demonstration in U.S. history within the grounds of the White House took place today in 1841 when President John Tyler got a bit too big for his boots. The newly appointed man at the top had vetoed a Bill and ***his opponents the Whig party wanted a fight****.*

16th August

The Dole Air Race race took place today in 1927 where competitors had to fly from California to Honolulu in the fastest time. Of the eight aircraft who started to race two crashed on take-off, two returned for repairs, two crashed in the Pacific ***and just two made it to Honolulu.***

16th August

The life of Elvis Presley came to an untimely end in the early hours of this morning in 1977 and the world was in shock. The King of Rock 'n' Roll had sung his final song and his Graceland mansion has since become a shrine to the ***thousands of fans who visit every year.***

17th August

It was this very afternoon in 1896 that a lady named Bridget Driscoll became the first person ever to be fatally wounded in a car accident. Bridget was crossing the road in the grounds of the Crystal Palace when she was ***run over by a Benz travelling at less than 7mph****.*

17th August

An earthquake struck southwestern Montana this August afternoon in 1959 destroying much of the habitat and killing 28 people. In it's wake a body of water appeared which was 6 miles long and 190 feet deep and as ***it was clearly there to stay it was named Quake Lake.***

17th August

The life of convicted Nazi Rudolph Hess ended today in 1987 after 46 years in captivity. Hess had been locked up in the Tower of London before spending his final years as the only inmate of the infamous Spandau Prison and ***soon after his death the prison was demolished****.*

17th August

Born this August day in Manhattan NYC 1943 was Hollywood actor Robert De Nero who shot to stardom following his portrayal of Vito Corleone in Godfather II. His movie performances are so legendary that British pop group ***Bananarama even sang a song about him****.*

18th August

In an unimaginable and shocking act a mother murdered her own 1-year old son today in Newfoundland 2003 after being given custody of him by the courts. The baby boy was Zachary Turner and his mother was already facing ***trial for the murder of Zachary's father****.*

18th August

*The Battle of Britain was going full throttle when the Luftwaffe made an all out effort to destroy RAF Fighter Command today in 1940 but they failed in their assault. Both sides lost more aircraft today than any other during **the fierce engagement known as - The Hardest Day***

18th August

*The nineteenth amendment to the American constitution was finally introduced today in 1920 and it gave women the right to vote. Consisting of just 27 words this became the shortest amendment of them all but **it's ratification meant so much to so many.***

18th August

*Hollywood heart-throb Patrick Swayze was born this August day in 1952 and amongst the many great movies in which he starred were Ghost and Dirty Dancing. During his lifetime Patrick became so famous that at the age of 39 **was voted the 'Sexiest Man Alive'**.*

18th August

*Born this August day in 1936 California USA was movie legend Robert Redford who has numerous acting awards to his name. This one time Hollywood Heartthrob starred in many great films and one of the most memorable Just **has to be Butch Cassidy and the Sundance Kid.***

19th August

It was this August day in 1839 the French government purchased a patent no: 8194 and promptly announced the invention a Free Gift to the World. Because of this gift today is known as World Photography Day so ***get your cameras out and start sharing those pictures.***

19th August

Three years on from Sputnik 1&2 the Russians charged off into Space again today in 1960 with another Sputnik launch. There were plenty of 'passengers' on board in the form of 2 Dogs, 40 Mice, 2 Rats and even a variety of plants ***but there were no human beings.***

19th August

Born this day in 1946 was a boy who grew up to become William Jefferson Clinton the 42nd President of America. Bill had quite a colourful time in office and after famously declaring "I did not have sexual relations with ***that woman" he was nicknamed Slick Willy.***

19th August

Gabrielle 'Coco' Chanel was born today in 1883 and she grew to become a world leader in fashion and perfume with her most famous brand being Chanel No5. Coco lived her life her way and was a highly successful businesswoman ***but she was also a Nazi collaborator.***

19th August

Hungerford has long been a quiet little market town out in the scenic countryside of Berkshire. Then on this August day in 1987 an act of terror struck like never before when a gunman armed with a semi-automatic rifle ***mercilessly killed 16 people before killing himself.***

20th August

It was one day after the death of Emperor Augustus that his maternal grandson Agrippa Postumus who had been in exile was executed by his own guards in mysterious circumstances. The guards had decided to wait for Augustus to die ***before they murdered his grandson.***

20th August

On this sunny August afternoon in 1672 the Prime Minster of Holland was attacked then murdered by a frenzied mob and after killing him they tried to eat him. This PM's name was Johan-de-Witt and no one was ever ***caught, questioned or charged with his murder.***

20th August

The Massacre at Ayyadieh took place today in 1191 when King Edward I had over 2,000 Muslim prisoners of war be-headed in front of the watching Saladin forces. Saladin responded with a counter-massacre and ***executed the 2,300 Christians he had captured.***

20th August

One stressed out postal worker in Oklahoma had just about had enough today in 1986 and was at the end of his tether but what he did next shocked a nation. He marched into work with a firearm and gunned-down ***14 of his colleagues and then shot and killed himself****.*

20th August

Winston Churchill told the nation that "Never in the field of human conflict was so much owed by so many to so few" today in 1940 and made sure everyone knew of the ongoing courage and bravery of RAF pilots ***fighting the Luftwaffe in the ongoing Battle of Britain****.*

21st August

The Mona Lisa was stolen this August day in 1911 and although Picasso got the blame the culprit was a Louvre employee of Italian descent. For 3 years the famous painting was missing over and 2,000 people visited the Louvre ***to see where this work of art had been****.*

21st August

Born today in Jamaica 1986 was Olympic Gold medalist and record breaker Usain Bolt. This incredible athlete who is the fastest man in the world named his daughter Olympia Lightning Bolt and once said ***" You have to learn how to lose before you can learn how to win"****.*

21st August

Russian politician Leon Trotsky died today in 1940 after being stabbed in the skull with an Ice-pick by a KGB agent acting on orders from Joseph Stalin. Years later Punk-Rockers The Stranglers made reference to the assassination ***with their hit single - No more Heroes****.*

21st August

A physicist named Henry Daghlian was carrying out an experiment with Demon Core today in 1945 when disaster befell him. He was fatally irradiated during the experiment at the Los Alamos National Laboratory New Mexico ***in what they called a criticality accident.***

21st August

Celebrated Country artist Kenny Rogers was born this August day in 1933 and was just another country singer until one song launched him to Superstardom. He never looked back after the world heard him sing those words - ***You picked a fine time to leave me Lucille.***

22nd August

This August day in 1485 was a long time coming for Henry Tudor and as he marched his army onto Bosworth field to do battle his sole aim was to destroy the Yorkists and become King of England. He got his wish and Henry VII is ***the only King to be Crowned on the battlefield****.*

22nd August

Many battles have taken place through the ages between England and Scotland and today in 1138 the Battle of the Standard took place in Yorkshire. King David I of Scotland crossed the border to do battle but was defeated by ***the English in the slaughter that followed****.*

22nd August

The nemonic 'Richard Of York Gave Battle In Vain' dates back to this very day in 1485 when the Battle of Bosworth was fought between Henry Tudor and King Richard III. The King was slain during the battle and his body found beneath ***a Leicester car park over 500 years later***

22nd August

As Britain attempted to attack Quebec from the seas today in 1711 during Quebec Expedition the assault went horribly wrong when the force of nature struck. Over 850 soldiers, sailors and women went to a watery grave in ***one of the worst naval disasters in British history.***

22nd August

The Year was 1642 and tensions in England were running high between Parliamentarians and Royalists when King Charles I rode into Nottingham today and defiantly raised the Royal Standard. This act signalled ***the beginning of a long and bloody English civil war****.*

23rd August

*The Beatles released 'She Loves You' today in 1963 and the song became another chart topper for the Fab Four as well as their best-selling single. When songwriting credits were published they read Lennon-McCartney **for the first time and stayed that way ever since**.*

23rd August

*A Royal Wedding ceremony took place this glorious August afternoon in 1200 when King John of England married Isabella of Angoulême and made her his Queen consort. During their 16 year marriage the couple **had 5 children one of whom was the future King Henry III.***

23rd August

*The Battle of Stalingrad started today in 1943 during WWII and raged for over 5 months through a bitter Russian winter. Germany, Italy, Romania and Hungary fought the Soviet Union and the two million casualties made this **one of the bloodiest battles in warfare history**.*

23rd August

*Sir William Wallace was executed today in 1305 at Smithfield London on the orders of English King Edward I during the Wars of Scottish independence. The Scottish leader was hanged, drawn, quartered, decapitated and **then buried in an unmarked grave in London**.*

24th August

It was during the Second war of American Independence hundreds of British troops went on the rampage today in 1814 tearing their way through Washington DC. With little resistance against them the men were hell bent ***on destruction and set fire to the White House.***

24th August

It was this August day in 1349 in the town of Mainz in Germany on the Rhine river that 6,000 innocent Jews were brought together and executed. The Bubonic plague had taken hold resulting in severe loss of life and sadly it was ***the Jewish population who got the blame.***

24th August

Sean Connery was born this warm August day in 1930 Edinburgh and was propelled to superstardom in his first James Bond 007 role after saying yes to Dr No. During his Navy days Sean acquired 2 tattoos one read ***Mum & Dad and the other read Scotland Forever.***

24th August

Sixteen years before the Hindenburg disaster the British owned Zeppelin R-38 was up in the skies today when disaster struck. An explosion sent the airship crashing down into Humber estuary and the number of ***lives lost was greater than those lost on Hindenburg****.*

24th August

*It was known as the 'Panic of 1857' and it all started this very day in that very year. Prior to this the US economy had been fruitful but poor investments spelt big trouble and the reason the panic spread so rapidly is because **Samuel Morse had just invented the Telegraph**.*

25th August

*The Liberation of Paris took place today in 1944 after more than 4 years of Nazi occupation during WWII. An uprising led by the French with help from Allies was relentless and after 6 bloody days of battle the German **garrison, outnumbered and outfought surrendered**.*

25th August

*British troops were running riot in the USA this August day in 1814 during the second war of independence. They set fire to the Library of Congress, United States Treasury, Department of War and many other public buildings **on day 2 of the Burning of Washington DC.***

25th August

*Englishman Matthew Webb became the first person to swim the English Channel when he did so this August day in 1875. This was Matthew's second attempt and he swam England to France but the current was so strong **he had to zig-zag his way across the waves**.*

26th August

The Battle of Crécy took place today in 1346 and English King Edward III and his men were victorious against the French despite being well outnumbered. But Crécy was just a small part of the long and bloody conflict between these ***two countries that lasted over 100 years.***

26th August

The Mini motorcar first appeared today in 1959 and became a true 20th century cultural icon. The car has many faces these days but only the original Mini conjures up images of a red, white and blue car chase the ***Self Preservation Society all that Gold in the Italian Job.***

26th August

The Magician and Escape Artist Harry Houdini wowed the crowds again today in 1907 with another astonishing piece of escapism. The magic man was locked in chains then submerged deep under water in an Aquatic Park ***and 57 seconds later he escaped a watery grave****.*

27th August

The deadliest attack on British Forces by the IRA in Northern Ireland took place this August day in 1979 when 18 soldiers were killed in an ambush. Then later the same day an IRA bomb planted in a boat was detonated and ***killed British Royal Lord Mountbatten and 3 others.***

27th August

The eruption of Krakatoa this morning in 1883 was the loudest noise ever heard by man. The self destruction of Krakatoa had devastating consequences and although this great mountain has gone, another now grows in it's place ***and is aptly named - Child of Krakatoa.***

28th August

Pizza delivery driver Brian Wells was murdered today in 2003 when an explosive collar around his neck detonated and blew his head off during a complex bank robbery. The horrific incident was actually shown on live television ***and became known as 'Pizza Bomber Case'****.*

28th August

One of the most famous speeches in the world was given this very afternoon in 1963 right in front of the Abraham Lincoln statue in Washington DC. Thousands of people stood and listened as Martin Luther King stood up ***and spoke the words ' I have a dream........'***

29th August

When the Olympic Marathon of 2004 took place today today the race followed the same route as it did at the first modern Olympic Games 108 years earlier. The athletes ran the race from the historic site of the Battle of ***Marathon to the Panathenaic Stadium in Athens.***

29th August

The Beatles played their final ever concert this Very night in 1966 when the Fab Four dazzled fans at the Candlestick Park stadium in San Francisco. Although 25,000 tickets were sold for the gig there were still another ***7,000 available tickets that were never sold****.*

30th August

Melbourne was founded today in Australia 1835 and was named after the British Prime Minster at the time who served his Majesty King William IV. The city of Melbourne later became the capital of the new Australian Colony ***named in honour of our Queen Victoria****.*

30th August

The British Royal Navy 24-gun HMS Pandora sank without trace this day in 1791 after running aground on the Great Barrier Reef 2 days earlier. She had famously hunted down the Bounty mutineers and is one of the most ***significant shipwrecks in the Southern Hemisphere.***

31st August

It was the early hours of this morning in 1997 that Princess Diana lost her life following a fatal car crash in a road tunnel in Paris when the Mercedes Benz in which she was a passenger was being pursued by Paparazzi. The world was ***soon in mourning for the People's Princess***

31st August

A 'False Flag' attack took place this evening in 1939 when German radio station Glewitz came under fire with the attackers posing as Polish nationals. In retaliation Nazi Germany Hitler invaded Poland the next morning in ***the full knowledge the Nazis staged the attack***

September

Taken from the Latin 'Septem' meaning Seven as September started life as the Seventh Month of the Year

This is one of the Four Months of the Year with 30 Days and is also the Month of the Year with the Longest Name

The Day that Ends the Month of September is always Different to the Day that Ends Any other Month in the Year

Following The Autumn Equinox in September Each Year the Dark of the Night lasts longer than the Daylight

The Birthstone For September is the Diamond and the Two Signs of the Zodiac are Virgo and Libra

September is Dedicated to Vulcan the Roman God of Fire who Ended up Marrying Venus the Goddess of Beauty

They call the Full Moon of September the Corn Moon as this is the Time for Gathering the Main Crops of Corn

Thirteen Days Disappeared from September when Britain Adopted the Gregorian Calendar - And all Hell Broke Loose

That's a Fact !!

1st September

In the World Chess Championship of 1972 Boris Spassky faced Bobby Fischer in Reykjavik. The men were to resume play this morning and complete game 21 but Spassky resigned without moving one chess piece and Fischer won this ***'Match of the Century' by 4 clear points.***

1st September

It was two years on from the invention of the telephone on this sunny September morning in 1878 that the world's first female telephone operator was appointed. The very capable young lady was recruited by Alexander Graham ***Bell himself and her name was Emma Nutt.***

2nd September

A fire that started in a bakery in Pudding Lane tonight in 1666 turned so ferocious it destroyed over 10,000 buildings, consumed St Paul's Cathedral and caused the death of six people. Although the Great Fire of London had struck ***the good news was - It killed most of the Rats.***

2nd September

During the Napoleonic Wars the British had to stop anyone from helping Napoleon extend his task force. So today in 1807 in an effort to stop Denmark surrendering its fleet to the French Emperor the Royal Navy ***bombarded Copenhagen with fire bombs and rockets****.*

3rd September

The ferocious Battle of the Atlantic started this very day in 1939 as Britain declared war on Germany and this was the longest military campaign of WWII lasting 5 years 8 months and 5 days. The deadly battle finally ended in ***victory for the Allies on VE Day in 1945.***

3rd September

The Coronation of a King of England took place this September day in 1189 and it was the warrior Richard the Lion-Heart who took to the throne. Sadly a number of Jewish dignitaries who had brought gifts for the new King ***were attacked, stripped, whipped and murdered.***

4th September

Thirty years of bloodshed between the U.S Cavalry and American Indians had already passed when Geronimo found himself facing 5,000 cavalry today in 1886 at Skeleton Canyon. The great Indian leader knew he could ***surrender or die so wisely chose the former****.*

4th September

The opening ceremony for Scotland's Forth Road Suspension Bridge joining Edinburgh to Fife took place today in 1964 and it was Queen Elizabeth II with the Duke of Edinburgh who cut the ribbon. It's length of 8,241 feet made ***it the longest bridge in the world at the time****.*

4th September

The internet based search engine we all know as Google was founded this day in 1998 and has been a global phenomenon. But the name Google is actually a typo as the company should have been called Googol but ***somebody made a mistake and typed Google.***

5th September

A baby boy born today in Zanzibar in 1946 grew up to be the charismatic frontman of Supergroup Queen the one and only Freddie Mercury. At the time that Freddie joined the group they were called Smile so the ***first thing he did was change the name to Queen.***

5th September

It was during the Olympic Games in Rome 1960 a young man named Clay won Gold today in the light-heavyweight boxing competition. He would later turn professional, move to heavyweight, change his name to Muhammad Ali - ***Then float like a butterfly and sting like a bee****.*

5th September

It was this September evening at the 1972 Munich Summer Olympics the Palestinian terrorist group 'Black September' attacked, kidnapped then murdered eleven Israeli athletes. Despite this terror attack the I.O.C. decided ***between themselves - The games must go on.***

6th September

So who was the King who hid up a tree ? That was the future King Charles II who took refuge atop an Oak Tree today in Shropshire 1651 to escape Cromwell's Roundheads. In celebration of his momentous escape many ***pubs across the country are named the 'Royal Oak'.***

6th September

In a despicable act of absolute evil a group of poachers in Hwange National Park Zimbabwe poisoned Forty One unsuspecting African elephants today in 2003 after lacing their water cyanide. Sadly they didn't stop there ***and many more defenceless elephants would die****.*

6th September

The iconic ship The Mayflower famously set sail from Plymouth today in 1620 with 102 Pilgrims aboard en route to the New World America. After two miserable months at sea they anchored in Cape Cod to face ***the most severe winter they had ever known****.*

7th September

The daughter of Henry VIII and Anne Boleyn was born today in 1533 and her father was none too pleased as he wanted a son and heir to his kingdom Hen 25 years later and against all the odds this baby girl became Queen ***Elizabeth I and was the very last Tudor Monarch.***

7th September

Brazil declared independence from Portugal today in 1822 amidst chaos and conflict but the people of the country rejoiced. This had been a very long wait since an explorer named Pedro had discovered Brazil over three hundred ***years earlier claiming her for Portugal.***

7th September

Cunard passenger liner RMS Lusitania set sail on her maiden voyage this September evening in 1907 when she left Liverpool and headed for New York. And a crowd of over 200,000 people gathered to watch the largest passenger liner ***in the world sail away into the night.***

8th September

The notorious Boyd Gang of Toronto were a media favourite due to the sensational ways in which they carried out their crimes. So when the gang escaped from a prison cell this September night in 1952 the Canadian ***Broadcasting Corporation filmed the whole thing.***

8th September

A King in the making arrived this Autumn afternoon in 1157 and was the first born son of Henry II and Eleanor of Aquitaine. He became known as Richard the Lion Heart but during his ten year reign this King was always ***away crusading so spent very little time in England****.*

9th September

When William the Conquer died today at his castle in France in 1087 his body was left abandoned as his men deserted him. William had ruled England since his victory at Hastings but a fall from his horse had proved fatal ***for the King who had led the Norman invasion****.*

9th September

William Rufus ascended to the English throne today in 1087 following the death of his father William the Conquerer. The new King decided he would be known as William II and that's way it stayed until he was killed in the ***New Forest 13 years later most probably by his brother****.*

10th September

Terror struck beneath the waves near Norway today in 1939 when British submarines were on patrol and HMS Oxley was accidentally Torpedoed by HMS Triton. The lost crew of Oxley are commemorated today with the ***Dundee International Submarine Memorial****.*

10th September

The Guillotine was the preferred form of execution in France during the French Revolution where even Louis XVI and Marie Antoinette lost their heads. But it was this September day 1977 this Blade of Death was ***last used In Paris to execute a convicted murderer.***

10th September

*The most famous **three seconds** in Olympic history were played out today in 1972 when Russians beat America to take Gold in Basketball. The Americans were so incensed they refused to accept the result and to this day have **never collected their nice shiny Silver medals.***

11th September

*"There is no fancy way to say that I have sinned" declared President Bill Clinton today in 1998 when he finally admitted his relationship with Monica Lewinski. Although this teflon-kid managed to hang on to his Presidency **he did earn himself the nickname Slick Willy.***

11th September

*American Airlines flight 11 and United Airlines flight 175 crashed into the Twin Towers WTC, United Airlines flight 93 crashed to the ground in Pennsylvania and American Airlines Flight 77 crashed into the Pentagon. **The 9/11 terror attacks in 2001 can never be forgotten**.*

11th September

*Terrorists attacked America this morning in 2001 using hi-jacked planes full of passengers as missiles. The tragic events caused the destruction of the iconic Twin Towers in Manhattan and thousands of lives were lost as **the World watched in shock on 9/11.***

12th September

In the early hours of this morning in 1971 a team of bank robbers got away with over £1.5m in cash from Lloyds Bank in London. The crime took place in Baker Street and the cheeky thieves left a note saying the police would need to ***call on Sherlock Holmes to solve the case.***

12th September

The largest margin of victory in a legitimate game of professional football was witnessed this afternoon in 1885 Bonnie Scotland. Two teams took to the field and after the ref blew the whistle it was all out attack by ***Arbroath as they destroyed Bon Accord 36 – 0.***

12th September

Born this September day in 1944 was Barry White who grew up to find himself caught on the wrong side of the law. Whilst in prison serving time for crime Barry heard "Its now or never" being sung by Elvis and it was this song ***that inspired him to change his life forever.***

13th September

The Year was 122 AD and Roman Emperor Hadrian started building a brick wall today which stretched across England West to East. Roman Emperors are remembered for many things such as murder, madness and tyranny but ***Hadrian will always be remembered for his wall.***

13th September

Britain and France are separated by just 21 miles of water and the two countries have fought many battles over the centuries. One such battle took place today in 1759 during the Seven Years War and victory went to the British ***in the Battle of the Plains of Abraham****.*

13th September

Today was the last of the eleven days that 'disappeared' from our year in 1752 as Britain moved away from the Julian calendar and officially adopted the Gregorian calendar that we use today. But the British public were ***not happy and there were riots in the streets****.*

14th September

Theodore Roosevelt became the 26th and youngest ever President of the United States following the assassination of William McKinley today in 1901. Teddy was very popular and one of his hunting trips inspired the making of ***a little cuddly toy named Teddy Bear.***

14th September

Amy Winehouse was born today in London 1981 and at a young age became a singing phenomenon with fans across the globe. But Amy would pay a high price for her fame and fortune and like many before her, this singing superstar ***would become a member of the '27 Club'****.*

14th September

A Royal Australian Navy submarine HMAS AE1 out on patrol today in 1914 sank without trace killing all onboard. The submarine had dived and was flooded due to an insecure valve and 13 searches followed before she was ***found 103 years later and declared a war grave.***

15th September

The Lehman Brothers investment bank sent shock waves across the financial world this September day in 2008 after declaring the largest filing for Bankruptcy in US history. This giant had traded for over 158 years and its action today ***was followed by a Global Financial Crisis.***

15th September

The monumental battle of the skies that was fought between Great Britain and Germany during WWII reached a pivotal stage today in 1940 as Britain gained a major advantage. The Luftwaffe were no match for the RAF ***and today we celebrate Battle of Britain day.***

15th September

The official opening ceremony of the Liverpool to Manchester railway line took place this day in 1830 but was not without incident. An MP named William Huskisson who was quite accident prone tripped over on the track ***and was killed by Stephenson's Rocket.***

15th September

One of the most famous people ever to put pen to paper was born today in 1890 Torquay. With over two billion copies of her books sold across the globe she is recognised by Guinness Book of Records as the ***best-selling fiction writer of all time*** *-* ***Dame Agatha Christie.***

16th September

Nazi leader Adolf Hitler, the personification of evil, was at it again this September day in 1941. WWII wasn't going quite his way so he made one of his big announcements and declared that for every German killed ***then 100 Yugoslav people would be put to death.***

16th September

Born this September day in 1927 was Peter Falk and he became best known for playing dishevelled Los Angeles TV detective Lieutenant Columbo. In this much loved cop show Columbo always got his man (or woman) and all he ever ***needed was 'Just one more thing'.***

16th September

It was this day in 1498 the life of Tomás de Torquemada the brutal 'Grand Inquisitor' of the Spanish Inquisition finally ended. Over 300 years later Torquemada's tomb was ransacked and it is believed the remains of ***his skeleton were stolen, crushed and incinerated****.*

16th September

A world first in technology took place this day in 1959 New York which revolutionised document-copying forever and thousands of people watching couldn't believe their eyes. A company named Xerox completed a demonstration ***on live TV of the Xerox 914 photocopier****.*

17th September

The world's first airplane fatality took place this September afternoon in 1908 when Lieutenant Thomas Selfridge was killed in a plane crash. Orville Wright was at the controls of the Wright Flyer when the plane faltered and ***after 7 weeks in hospital Orville was alright.***

17th September

The Battle of Antietam took place today in 1862 during the American Civil War ending in marginal victory for the Abraham Lincoln's Union army. With over 22,000 lives lost, this was the bloodiest single day of this war and ***the first battle to take place on Union soil.***

17th September

The Battle of Britain had raged for over two months and the Allies were finally outgunning the Luftwaffe when the Nazis declared the abandonment of Operation Sea-Lion today in 1940 which meant that Hitler's planned ***Invasion of England was completely abandoned.***

17th September

It was on this September day in 1916 during the bloody Battle of the Somme in WWI that Tanks were first used in battle. It was the British armed forces who introduced this all new powerful addition to their arsenal making ***good use of their fire power to repel the Nazis.***

18th September

George I from the House of Hanover arrived in Britain from Germany today in 1714 to claim his crown as the country's new King. Reigning for almost 13 years he never spoke a word of English but was cruel enough to have ***his wife locked away in a castle until her death.***

18th September

One of the funniest sketches on TV aired this evening in 1976 and it showed two men struggling to communicate. If you haven't seen it, it's well worth seeing and if you have seen it, it's well worth seeing again the ***Two Ronnies with their four candles or fork handles.***

18th September

A Geyser in Yellowstone Park spouting boiling hot water high into the air at regular intervals today in 1870 was observed by an expedition party. The men were so fascinated by this force of nature they named the geyser 'Old Faithful' ***and she is still blowing strong to this day.***

19th September

The world famous Glastonbury Festival premiered this September day and into the evening in 1970 with tickets priced £1 each. It lasted one day and was titled the 'Pilton Pop, Folk & Blues Festival'. Headline act were the Kinks ***but they cancelled so in came Marc Bolan & T-Rex.***

19th September

Come On Let's Twist Again, Like We Did Last Summer, Let's Twist Again, Like We Did Last Year..... This almighty tune topped the charts today in 1960 and incredibly it seemed Chubby Checker had gotten everyone, everywhere, ***singing, dancing and doing the 'Twist'.***

19th September

Twentieth American President James A. Garfield finally succumbed the assassins bullet today in 1881 and became the second President to be assassinated. The fatal shot meant his time at the top was short lived and these days ***Garfield has is more widely known as a cat.***

20th September

Theodore Roosevelt was sworn in as the 21st President of the United States of America this sunny September morning in 1881 and in doing so he became the youngest person ever to take office. Theodore said his way to success was ***to " Talk calmly and carry a big stick".***

20th September

The Battle of Marathon concluded today in 490 BC as the Greeks defeated the mighty Persians. A man named Philippides ran the 26 miles from Marathon to Athens to tell of the victory and although he died of exhaustion ***when he got there, he left one hell of a legacy.***

20th September

Two ships collided today on the straits of the River Solent in 1911 and one was HMS Hawke with the other being the White Star ocean liner Olympic. The ships stayed afloat but were both badly damaged and the subsequent enquiry ***found no blame attached to HMS Hawke****.*

21st September

The United Nations declared September 21st the International day of Peace and that isn't such a bad thing. Just how many nations actually recognise this day of peace is another story altogether and that isn't such a good thing but ***someone once said "Give peace a chance".***

21st September

Infamous outlaw and Highwayman Dick Turpin was born today in 1705 and it wasn't long before he turned to a life of crime. Turpin fled north ending up near Harrogate under the assumed alias John Palmer but this man's ultimate ***destiny would be the hangman's noose****.*

21st September

The highly successful barrister, businessman and locksmith Cecil Chubb attended an auction today in 1915 Salisbury where he bought the Stonehenge monument for £6,000. Cecil gave it to his wife as a present but ***she refused it so he later gave it as a gift to the nation.***

22nd September

It was during the early days of WWI a German submarine beneath the waves with torpedoes at the ready went after 3 British cruisers firing on them. Seventy minutes later all 3 ships were under water and 1,500 sailors ***had lost their lives as the U-Boat sailed away****.*

22nd September

Abraham Lincoln stood tall today in 1862 and gave notice that his Emancipation Proclamation was soon to be introduced to the nation. He'd been waiting for the right moment to make his announcement and victory at Antietam ***5 days earlier gave him just that moment****.*

22nd September

When the Coronation of George III took place today in 1761 nobody knew he would end up becoming the longest reigning King in the history of the British Monarchy. Neither did they know that he would lose two wars ***against the Americans and end up going Mad.***

23rd September

It was during the Wars of the Roses the bloody Battle of Blore Heath took place today in 1459 and victory went to the House of York. The decisive moment in the Battle came during intense fighting when the Lancastrian Lord Audley ***was slain by Yorkist Sir Roger Kynaston.***

23rd September

Born this September day in 63 BC was a boy named Octavian and he grew up to become an all conquering Roman warrior. After ruthlessly dispatching Anthony & Cleopatra in battle he became the first Emperor of his beloved ***Rome and changed his name to Augustus.***

23rd December

Born this September day in Cookstown Ireland 1869 was a girl named Mary Mallon who grew up to be a cook and a killer. Although the latter was never deliberate Mary was an asymptotic disease carrier who infected many ***and so became known as Typhoid Mary.***

24th September

We all take a wrong turn now and then but today in 1972 Japanese Airlines Flight 472 to India landed in the wrong airport. The aeroplane overshot the runway as passengers screamed with fright but there were no casualties ***apart from the plane which had to be written off.***

24th September

Sadly no longer with us but born this September day in Liverpool 1942 was a boy who formed a band during the Merseybeat era and took their first three singles all to the very top of the charts. Gerry Marsden is his name ***and his message - You'll Never Walk Alone.***

25th September

Ford Motor Company founder Henry Ford introduced the 8 hours a day 5 days a week today in 1926 to the delight of his workforce. Henry Ford knew that if his men did what they should do when they should do it ***then he would achieve what he wanted to achieve.***

25th September

It was during The Troubles in Northern Ireland this day in 1983 that a break-out took place from the notorious Maze Prison in Belfast. Thirty-eight IRA prisoners armed with a number of handguns hijacked a prison food lorry ***then smashed their way to the outside world.***

26th September

After 3 days of play the world's first official international game of any sport concluded today in 1844 and cricket was the name of the game. Billed as 'United States of America-v-The British Empire's Canadian Province' - ***Canada beat the USA before they could say..... Howzat !!***

26th September

If this September day is the day you were born then you share your birthday with more people than anyone else on any other day of the year. More babies are born on this date in the year than on any other and the reason for ***this uniqueness is quite simple - It's Christmas !!***

27th September

George Stephenson's Locomotion No1 became the world's first passenger steam train today in 1835 when it choo chooed along the track packed packed with people. Many of whom were terrified when the train reached ***a white-knuckle-riding top speed of 27 mph.***

27th September

The Year was 1066 and while King Harold II of England was far from London fighting the Scots and Vikings another battle was looming. William the Conqueror set sail with his army today from the mouth of the Somme river ***to begin the Norman Conquest of England.***

28th September

Just 3 days after victory at the Battle of Stamford Bridge the life of King Harold II was again under threat today in 1066 with the news that his sworn enemy William Duke of Normandy had arrived on English soil in Sussex ***and was marching his army to Hastings.***

28th September

Sibling rivalry boiled over big time this day in 1106 and a right Royal fight ensued. England's Henry I led an army against his rebellious brother Robert at Tinchebray and victory for the King meant Robert was dragged away ***and locked up in Cardiff Castle until his death.***

29th September

An unimaginable moment of horror in the blues skies above Brazil took place today in 2006 when two flights turned to terror as a mid-air collision took place killing 154 people. The immediate aftermath of this terrible ***disaster triggered a Brazilian aviation crisis.***

29th September

A boy born this September day in 1941 grew up to be an evil killer who's shocking crimes caught up with him when bodies of his victims were found at his home in Gloucester. This evil killer was Fred West and his home in ***Cromwell Street has now been demolished****.*

30th September

In the town of Bedrock a page right out of history hit small screens this afternoon in 1960 as the Flintstones made their TV debut. The famous family were watched by millions and Fred and Wilma became the first couple ***to be shown on TV in bed – Yabba-dabba-doo !!***

30th September

If you remember the Glam-Rock era you will remember Marc Bolan who gave us Telegram Sam, Ride a White Swan and Metal Guru to name but a few. Marc was born today in 1947 but tragically died in a car crash exactly ***two weeks before he would turn 30 years old.***

October

Taken from the Latin and Greek for Eight - October became the Tenth Month of the Year when Two more were Added

October is one of the 7 Months of the Year with 31 Days but is has 745 Hours Making it the Longest Month of them all

The World Famous Oktoberfest Lasts 16 - 18 Days and Always Finishes on the First Sunday in October

Halloween is Celebrated this Month to Remember the Dead including Saints, Martyrs and dearly Departed

October is a Month of Sunshine and Warmth in The Southern Hemisphere where Spring has finally Sprung

The Birthstone for the Month of October is the Opal and the Two Zodiac Signs are Libra and Scorpio

October is Usually the Month of the Hunter's Moon but this Moon Will Also Arrive Later When it Wants To

This Amazing Month will Celebrate Many an Event in Many an Amazing Way and That Includes - World Zombie Day

That's a Fact !!

1st October

The life of notorious gangland criminal Reggie Kray came to an end this October day in 2000 and he finally left his prison cell forever. Twin brother Ronnie died five years earlier and the two legends of London's gangland had ***spent most of their lives locked behind bars****.*

1st October

One billion viewers tuned in to watch a heavyweights boxing match tonight in 1975 when Smokin' Joe Frazier fought Muhammad Ali in their third and final fight. After 14 rounds both were out on their feet when Joe's corner threw in the towel ***to end the 'Thriller in Manilla'****.*

2nd October

HMS Curacoa was one of the escort ships supporting RMS Queen Mary off the Irish coast today in 1942 when she sailed too close to her Queen and was sliced in two. Accounts differ as to what actually happened next but ***what is clear is that 337 crewmen were killed****.*

2nd October

Born today in 1452 was England's future King Richard III and it was during his short reign that the Princes in the Tower disappeared. Thanks to William Shakespeare history has not been kind to the King who was slain at Bosworth ***and buried almost 530 years later.***

2nd October

This afternoon in 1976 the first Red Cards in English football were issued when two players were sent off. The men in question were Wagstaffe of Blackburn Rovers and a Fulham player who saw red that day for ***swearing at the Ref was a bloke named George Best.***

3rd October

The German Democratic Republic finally ended today in 1990 following the he destruction of the Berlin Wall and a new Germany was born. This German moment of reunification is now celebrated each year and has ***the not so dazzling title of German Unity Day.***

3rd October

A young Elvis Presley gave his first public performance this October day in 1945 when he was just ten years old after entering a local talent competition. The future King of Rock 'n' Roll had to settle for 5th place after ***singing the ballad about a dog named Old Shep****.*

3rd October

King of Pop Michael Jackson and ex-Beatle Paul McCartney released their new single Say, Say, Say today in the UK 1981 and fans flocked to buy it. At the time Michael actually owned the rights to the Beatles songs and ***over 30 years later Paul bought them all back.***

4th October

The Loomis Fargo Bank Robbery took place in North Carolina this 1997 evening as robbers got away with a cool $17.3 million in cold hard cash. Unfortunately for the bandits the FBI were on their tail and 24 people were soon ***inside for their part in 'the hillbilly heist'****.*

4th October

Pope Gregory XIII declared the Julian calendar outdated this day in 1582 and introduced his own Gregorian version. Many countries adopted the all new calendar straight away but another 170 years passed before Britain ***would follow suit and go the Gregorian way.***

4th October

Russia launched Sputnik 1 satellite today in 1957 to get ahead of America in the Space race and were very pleased with themselves. They then decided to go one better so announced plans to launch another Sputnik to ***leave the Americans feeling lost in space****.*

5th October

Born this October day in 1829 was the boy who became America's 21st President. He was Chester A. Arthur but he was one of those long forgotten Presidents until his name was the answer to a life saving question in ***one of the Bruce Willis Die Hard movies.***

5th October

Around 200 men set off from the North East on a long march to London today in 1936 demanding money and jobs. The 'Jarrow March' took 26 days to reach the capital where the men made their demands but ***all they got was their train fare back to Jarrow.***

5th October

Two years on from their historic first flight at Kitty Hawk the Wright Brothers were up in the skies again today in 1905 with more history in the making. The two high fliers flew their Wright Flyer III straight into the record books as ***they travelled 24 miles in just 39 minutes.***

6th October

The Great Fire of Newcastle & Gateshead started today in 1854 just after midnight and crowds started to gather as the fire spread. Suddenly there was one almighty explosion which shook everything in sight destroying ***hundreds of buildings and killing 53 people****.*

6th October

The life of a true legend of the Silver Screen came to an end this very day in 1989 with the passing Bette Davis. Recognised as one of Hollywood's greatest actresses Bette starred in so many movies that she was affectionately ***known as - The fourth Warner brother.***

6th October

The original Moulin Rouge opened for business this October evening in 1889 and its impact was immediate. The building had a giant Red Windmill on its roof and after accidentally burning down in 1915 Moulin Rouge ***was rebuilt and is the home of the Can-Can****.*

6th October

It was during Nazi Germany's invasion of Poland in 1939 that the 'September Campaign' was launched and Polish forces offered their tormentors little resistance. The relentless assault finally ended today when 17,000 ***Polish troops were captured at the Battle of Kock.***

7th October

Russian President Vladimir Putin born today 1952 is an expert in martial arts and seems to consider himself as a bit of a tough guy but he does have a sense of humour. He knew Angela Merkel was afraid of dogs so ***when he met her he took a couple of Dobermans along.***

7th October

The world's first airline KLM was founded today in 1919 in the Netherlands and has flown the flag of aviation ever since. The Dutch had wasted no time in taking to the skies as this was only sixteen years after the ***Wright brothers flew the world's first aeroplane.***

7th October

Born this October day in 1959 was the X Factor and Britains Got Talent guru Simon Cowell. Long before his fame on the talent shows Simon was a contestant on 'Sale of the Century' hosted by Nicholas Parsons and ***in case you're wondering – Yes Simon did win.***

7th October

In response to the appalling acts of terror on 9/11 the USA attacked Afghanistan tonight in 2001 launching 'Operation Enduring Freedom' US President George W Bush had given numerous ultimatums to the Taliban which ***had been ignored so now it was all out attack.***

8th October

The Great Chicago Fire started tonight in 1871 causing almost 300 fatalities and leaving 100,000 homeless. It started in O'Leary's barn but their house remained untouched throughout the blaze and the O'Leary family ***needed police protection when the blaze was over.***

8th October

The Year was 1974 and after a time of troubles and woes the Franklin National Bank of America suffered catastrophic collapse today. This was a direct result of fraud, bad management and greed and was at the time by far ***the largest bank failure in United States History.***

8th October

It was the day before his 31st birthday the world's most famous Beatle released 'Imagine' today in 1971 and it became one of the best selling singles in the world. Liverpool's John Lennon Airport pays tribute to their famous son ***with the greeting - Above us only Sky.***

8th October

The fire that raged through Peshtigo Wisconsin this October day in 1871 caused the deaths of over 2,000 people and destroyed hundreds of homes. But this tragic event is always overshadowed by another fire that started in a barn on ***the very same day in Chicago.***

9th October

Born this October day in 1926 was Ruth Ellis and she grew up to become the last woman in Britain ever to be receive the death penalty and be hanged. Ruth did have one thing in common with the last man hanged in ***Britain - They were both born in Rhyl.***

9th October

The Year was 1290 and three months after King Edward I had signed an order expelling of the entire Jewish population from England this was the day the last 16,000 Jews left the country. All debts owed to anyone in the ***Jewish community were now payable to the Crown.***

9th October

Born this October day in New York 1975 was a boy named Sean Taro Ono Lennon and he was the son of John and Yoko. Not so unusual or particularly relevant except for the fact that Sean was born exactly 35 years to the day ***after the birth of his famous father in 1940.***

9th October

Born this October day in 1940 was a boy named John Lennon who became world famous as one of the Beatles and also had a fabulous solo career. But the shocking assassination of the ex-Beatle in New York means Lennon ***has now been dead longer than he was alive.***

10th October

London Bridge was officially unveiled today in 1971 at an opening ceremony in Arizona USA. The Americans had bought and paid for the famous bridge then transported it across the Atlantic, rebuilt it brick by brick, added a river, some houses and created a town.

10th October

The worst nuclear disaster in the UK started today in 1957 at the power plant Windscale and the fire lasted 3 days. Rated 5 out of 7 on the International Nuclear Event Scale the long term death toll was 240 and ***the name of this place was later changed to Sellafield.***

10th October

From Russia With Love premiered in London today in 1963 and was Ian Fleming's second Bond movie to be shown on the big screen. This is the only Bond movie that features the name of a country in its title and the numbers ***007 just happen to be the dialling code for Russia.***

11th October

The year was 1937 and Edward and Mrs Simpson who were by now known as the Duke and Duchess of Windsor started a tour of Nazi Germany this cold October day. Their Royal tour lasted almost two weeks and ***culminated in a nice cozy meeting with Adolph Hitler.***

11th October

Oliver Cromwell and his New Model Army were out for blood today in 1649 and they would show no mercy. The Roundheads brutally attacked Wexford and didn't stop their onslaught until they had killed over 2,000 Irish ***confederate troops and murdered 1,500 civilians.***

11th October

King Henry VIII's great ship, the Mary Rose was raised from the seabed this day in 1982 and taken to Portsmouth. The combination of an inexperienced Captain, rough seas, excessive weight, strong winds and the French ***had caused her sinking over 400 years earlier****.*

11th October

Welcome to 'International Day of the Girl Child' which was founded this October day in 2012 by the United Nations in recognition of every girl everywhere. This international observance day highlights the real importance of ***equality and protection against discrimination.***

12th October

The shocking murder of two police officers in Victoria Australia took place today in 1988 during the early hours. The men were responding to reports of an abandoned vehicle when they were gunned down by cold-blooded killers ***who were arrested but somehow acquitted.***

12th October

In a despicable act of cruelty British nurse Edith Cavell was executed by German firing squad in Belgium this October morning in 1915 after being found guilty by court marshal of treason. The only thing Edith was guilty of ***was nursing wounded soldiers back to recovery.***

12th October

One of the most famous statues in the world was unveiled today in 1931 and it overlooks Rio de Janeiro in Brazil. Standing 98ft tall it is the statue of Christ the Redeemer and this magnificent sculpture is also recognised as ***one of the new Seven Wonders of the World.***

12th October

The baby boy born to Henry VIII and third wife Jane Seymour this day in 1537 meant this Tudor King finally had the son and heir he had been waiting for. When the boy took to the throne as King Edward VI 10 years later he was ***the country's first ever Protestant monarch.***

13th October

Liverpool's Fab Four played to a packed audience at the Palladium this October evening in 1963 and such was the hysteria surrounding the performance that no words could describe the event. A new word was needed ***and so the phrase 'Beatlemania' was born****.*

13th October

The U.S. Navy was founded today in 1775 and one of the reasons for its introduction to the high seas was to fight the British. America was preparing to declare it's independence from Britain and knew this declaration ***would have to be settled on land and at sea.***

13th October

Uruguayan Air Force Flight 571 bound for Santiago Chile crashed in the remote Andes Mountains and in order to stay alive survivors later turned to cannibalism and ate some of the dead. This crash happened in the October of 1972 ***and the day was Friday the Thirteenth****.*

13th October

Unlucky thirteen came calling for Roman Emperor Claudius this early morning in 54 AD and the man who succeeded the murdered Caligula was himself given a dose of poison that would kill him. Unsurprisingly it was his darling wife ***Agrippa who did the dirty deed.***

14th October

The most famous Battle ever fought on English soil took place this very day in 1066 and it lasted eight hours before King Harold II took an arrow in his eye and said goodbye. England had fallen to a French invasion led by ***William of Normandy in a town named Hastings.***

14th October

The Nobel Peace Prize was awarded this day in 1964 to Martin Luther King Jr. for 'combating racial inequality through nonviolence'. Nobel prizes are named after the inventor of dynamite Alfred Nobel whose foundation was created solely ***to reward those who serve humanity.***

14th October

Most people know the Battle of Hastings was in 1066 but the battle itself took place this very day and lasted the best part of eight hours. King Harold II was mortally wounded on the battlefield and his body had to be formally ***identified by his mistress Edith Swanneck.***

14th October

Forty four years after man's first flight at Kitty Hawk U.S. Air Force pilot Chuck Yeager flew faster than the speed of sound today in 1947 and became the first man ever to do so. Yeager flew his supersonic aircraft the ***Bell X-1 almost 1,500 mph at 45,000 feet.***

15th October

This morning in 1917 the actress, seductress and spy, Mata Hari was executed by French firing squad but this lady was defiant to the very end. Mata Hari turned away a nun, refused a blindfold, lit a cigarette and then ***blew the soldiers a kiss - just before they shot her.***

15th October

Edgar the AEthling was proclaimed King of England the day after the Battle of Hastings today in 1066 but William the Conqueror had other ideas. Within weeks this new King who was never crowned conceded power after deciding ***not to get involved in a fight he couldn't win****.*

15th October

She was a spy and seductress who lived life very dangerously and today in 1917 her ill-doings had finally caught up with her. The firing squad had fingers on triggers and had taken their aim but before they could shoot to ***kill Mata Hari she blew them a Kiss.***

15th October

A young Queen Victoria decided she needed a husband so today in 1839 she proposed to Germany's Prince Albert and the two were married four months later. During their marriage the two produced nine children and introduced England to the Christmas tree.

16th October

A baby boy born this October day in 1797 grew up to become Lord Cardigan who fearlessly led the Charge of the Light Brigade towards Russian cannons during the Crimean War. Cardigan had been despised in England but after this ***charge he became a national hero.***

16th October

There are many shows in tv's Soapland with avid viewers having their favourite and it was this early evening in 1972 that Emmerdale Farm hit the TV screens. These days the Farm has gone but Emmerdale lives on and ***this is the soap that started with a Funeral.***

16th October

The Importance of Being Ernest, A Woman of No Importance, Lady Windermere's Fan, An Ideal Husband, are just some of those instantly recognisable works of a famous Irish playwright born this very day in Dublin 1854 his name ***- Oscar Fingal O'Flahertie Wills Wilde.***

16th October

The literary Brontë classic Jane Eyre was published today in 1847 having been written by Charlotte under the pen name of Currer Bell. The novel enjoyed a wonderful reception as readers fell in love with the title character ***and were very much intrigued by Mr Rochester.***

17th October

The infamous Chicago mobster 'Al Capone' was convicted of tax evasion this very day in 1931 and then spent the next eight years in Alcatraz Penitentiary. The taxman caught Capone and that was something that **Elliot Ness and the Untouchables could never do***.*

17th October

Over 300,000 gallons of beer burst out of their giant wooden barrels today in 1814 and raced down Tottenham Court at a furious pace engulfing all in its path. So fierce was this onslaught of booze that 8 people were killed ***"casually, accidentally and by misfortune"****.*

17th October

Following the execution of his father eleven years earlier it was today in 1660 King Charles II tasted revenge when nine of the Regicides who had signed the death warrant of King Charles I were rounded up and each one of them ***mercilessly hung, drawn and quartered****.*

17th October

*Albert Einstein was a German citizen for over fifty years but following the rise of the Nazi party he fled the country today in 1933 never to return. The scientific genius lived the rest of his life in the USA and his formula E=mc2 has been **dubbed the world's most famous equation**.*

18th October

*Today in 1995 saw the end of the life of the four legged legend from Southport known to the world as Red Rum. This famous racehorse had won the Grand National three times and was runner-up twice lived to the age of thirty **is buried on the course at Aintree.***

18th October

*A boy named Lee born today in 1939 grew up, joined the US Marines, served his country and was virtually unknown. Then one November evening his name became known across the world but still to this day most Americans refuse to believe that **Lee Harvey Oswald killed JFK.***

18th October

*Born this October day in Belgium 1960 was a baby boy who grew up to be the Hollywood star who karate kicked his way through many a movie and always seemed to get the girl. This man of martial arts is known as **Jean-Claude Van Damme aka The Muscles from Brussels**.*

18th October

The freezing cold and mostly baron land of Alaska became part of USA today in 1867 after the Americans had purchased the land from Russia for just $7.2million. Alaska is the largest of the fifty states but it's population is ***less than the smallest State of Rhode Island****.*

19th October

The final land Battle in the War of Independence ended this day in 1781 at Yorktown with victory for America (helped by the French). The Battle had raged for 21 days and the outnumbered British troops led by Lord Cornwallis ***were left with two choices - Surrender or Die.***

19th October

Few wedding ceremonies in history have had an impact like the one that took place today in 1469 when Ferdinand II of Aragon married Isabella of Castile. After they tied the Royal knot their marriage led to the unification of ***Aragon and Castile which created Spain****.*

19th October

Maybe English composer Edward Elgar knew Liverpool would one day be the epicentre of the music world. As this was the city he chose today in 1901 to host the premiere of his most spectacular piece of work ***Elgars musical masterpiece - Pomp & Circumstance.***

19th October

It was in the early hours of this October morning in 1216 that the reign of King John came to an end following a feast of peaches and ale. The King who had reigned for seventeen years had a number of enemies and rumours ***soon spread that he had been poisoned****.*

20th October

When the plane in which rock band Lynyrd Skynyrd were travelling crashed today in 1977 the lead singer and guitarist both perished in the explosion. The band named themselves after their schoolteacher and their their most ***famous track was "Sweet home Alabama"****.*

20th October

The Brink's armed Robbery of 1981 took place today in Nanuet New York when members of the Black Liberation Army and the Weather Underground got away with $1.6 million. The gang were later caught but not before ***they murdered 2 police officers and a Brink's guard.***

20th October

Australia's world famous Sydney Opera House was officially opened this fine October day in 1973 by Queen Elizabeth II. Jørn Utzon had designed this magnificent structure but he hadn't been invited to the opening ceremony ***because he had resigned before completion****.*

20th October

Two months on from the passing of Queen Anne in 1714 King George was crowned in Westminster Abbey today and his arrival prompted riots across the country. He was 1st of four Georges from the House of Hanover who ***reigned for the next 116 years between them****.*

21st October

It was this morning in 1966 the most terrible tragedy struck in the small town of Aberfan in South Wales. The catastrophic collapse of a huge mountain of coal created a landslide which smothered a school causing the ***tragic loss of life of 16 adults and 128 children.***

21st October

"England expects every man will do his duty" declared Nelson today in 1805 ahead of the Battle of Trafalgar. The British won the battle but Horatio was fatally wounded on the deck of HMS Victory and his life ended aboard ***the ship that was built the year he was born.***

21st October

A shocking act of mass murder was carried out today in 1944 when French and Belgian POW's along with German civilians were brutally attacked and slaughtered by Russian Red Army soldiers. Women and children were also ***amongst the dead in the Nemmersdorf massacre.***

21st October

The Year was 1854 and nurse Florence Nightingale was sent with 38 staff to give medical attention to soldiers fighting in the Crimean war. Florence was eager to please and her incredible desire to do her duty made her one of ***the most famous nurses in the world.***

22nd October

Over 2,200 engineers and technicians along with their entire families and equipment were on the move today in 1946 as they went to live in the Soviet Union but this was not a move of choice. They'd all been forced ***at gunpoint to relocate from their homes in East Germany****.*

22nd October

A statue of the legendary Lady Godiva sitting naked upon her trusted horse Aethenoth was unveiled this morning in 1947 outside Coventry Town Hall. The statue commemorates Lady Godiva's famous journey through the town ***and was created by a man named William Dick.***

22nd October

High in the sky above Paris this calm October day in 1797 the world's first successful parachute jump was made by a Frenchman named André. People watched in amazement from the ground below as the Daredevil floated ***3,200 feet to the ground for a nice safe landing.***

22nd October

The FBI were having quite a year in 1934, they murdered Bonnie & Clyde, they put a bloody end to the life of John Dillinger and today was the turn of bank robber Pretty Boy Floyd, who they followed to Ohio where they ***shot and killed him in a town called East Liverpool****.*

23rd October

Throughout the ages battles have been given unusual names and today in 1739 was no exception. British Prime minister Sir Robert Walpole found himself at odds with the Spanish and so reluctantly started what ***is known as 'The war of Jenkins Ear'.***

23rd October

Born today in 1905 USA was a girl named Gertrude Ederle and she grew up to become an Olympic athlete who's specialist skills took place in the water. Then at the age of 21 this young Olympian became the ***first woman in the world to swim the English Channel.***

23rd October

Born this warm October day in 1940 Brazil was a true superstar from the world of sport. By the age of just 16 he was playing 'the beautiful game' for his country and is the only player ever to win 3 FIFA World Cup winning medals, ***always an ambassador and a gentleman - Pele****.*

23rd October

The Battle of Edge Hill took place today in 1642 and was the first battle of the English Civil War between Charles I Royalists and Cromwell's Parliamentarians. This result was inconclusive but 9 years of bloodshed would follow ***and it wouldn't end well for the King.***

24th October

Born this day in 1933 the notorious brothers who ruled London's gangland Kray twins Ronnie and Reggie. Although their reign of terror ended when they were 34 the 'terrible twins' remain a legend to many and are ***still the subject of book, film and television.***

24th October

Two boys born this October day in London 1933 would become the most infamous and notorious twins in living memory. Together they terrorised London's gangland with thuggery and murder and these terrible twins ***were known as Ronnie and Reggie Kray.***

24th October

When the George Washington bridge was ceremonially opened this October afternoon in 1931 it meant cars could finally cross the Hudson river. Thirty one years later another level was added to the bridge and today It's ***the busiest motor vehicle bridge in the world.***

25th October

A hot air balloon set off for the blue skies above France today in 1783 and although the untethered balloon finally had passengers on board they weren't human beings. This fatal flight lasted just over fifteen minutes and on board there ***were a Sheep, a Duck and a Monkey.***

25th October

Stormed at with shot and shell, Boldly they rode and well, Into the Jaws of Death, Into the Mouth of Hell, Rode the Six Hundred. Honour the charge they made, Honour the Light Brigade, Noble Six Hundred. This was 1854 during ***the Crimean War at the Battle of Balaclava.***

25th October

Liverpool's Anglican Cathedral was officially opened this day in 1978 and is the longest Cathedral in the world. This magnificent structure standing 331 ft tall was designed by Giles Gilbert Scott but the 74 yrs it took to construct meant ***Scott didn't live long enough to see it.***

26th October

The famous 'Pony Express' delivery service across America lasted 18 months before its abandonment today in 1861. If you were young, skinny and prepared to risk death on a daily basis you could ride the Pony Express but ***riders only ever rode a Horse and never a Pony.***

26th October

A fire started to blaze out of control today in 2003 killing 15 people and causing an incredible amount of damage as it blazed away destroying over 2,200 homes and 250,000 acres of land. This is the third largest in ***California history and they call it the Cedar Fire.***

26th October

The Year was 1863 and this October day witnessed the founding of the Football Association in England. This is the oldest association of its kind anywhere in the world although they don't seem to do much they do get to ***hire and fire the manager of England.***

27th October

When an America named Wallis Simpson got her divorce confirmed this October day in 1936 it spelt trouble for the British Monarchy. Wallis was getting set to snuggle up with Edward VIII but in order to be with her the King knew ***he would have to abdicate the throne.***

27th October

Remember to turn clocks and watches back tonight and gain an extra hour. British Summer Time officially ends early tomorrow morning when we revert back to Greenwich Mean Time and this single clock change gives October 745 hours making it the longest month of our year.

28th October

Americans Presidents seem to really like Liberty and Freedom and today in 1886 Grover Cleveland dedicated the Statue of Liberty which had been gifted to America by the French. Then on the same day fifty years later Franklyn ***Roosevelt dedicated the same statue again.***

28th October

Born today in 1967 America was the actress who's performance in a rom-com movie opposite Richard Gere 23 years later confirmed her as a Hollywood superstar. The must-see movie is a firm favourite and Julia Roberts is the ***Pretty Woman walking down the street.***

29th October

The Year was 1929 and hot on the heels of two brutal stock market crashes in America came another one today as the Great Recession took a stranglehold on the country. Billions of dollars had been lost and that ***spelt disaster for Herbert Hoover's presidency.***

29th October

Sir Walter Raleigh was executed this afternoon in 1618 on the orders of King James I and as he faced his death he shouted to the nervous axe-man 'Strike man Strike'! Raleigh's devoted wife Elizabeth claimed his severed head and ***kept it in her handbag for the next 29 years****.*

30th October

*The Coronation of England's first Tudor King took place this October morning in 1485 and it was Henry VII who wore the crown. He had combined the colours of the Houses of Lancaster and York to create his Tudor Rose and **all the new King needed now was a new Queen**.*

30th October

*Charismatic Hollywood actor Orson Welles took to the radio this October day in 1938 and read a story to the nation. His delivery of this work of fiction was so compelling that the shocked listeners really did believe **- the War of the World's had actually started.***

30th October

*The Coronation of England's first Tudor King took place this October morning in 1485 and it was Henry VII who wore the crown. He had combined the colours of the Houses of Lancaster and York to create his Tudor Rose and **all the new King needed now was a new Queen**.*

31st October

*The faces of four American Presidents unveiled today in 1941 show Washington, Jefferson, Lincoln and Roosevelt carved into Mount Rushmore. It was Gutzon Borglum who created this masterpiece but he died just **before completion and missed the opening ceremony**.*

31st October

The faces of four American Presidents unveiled today in 1941 show Washington, Jefferson, Lincoln and Roosevelt carved into Mount Rushmore. It was Gutzon Borglum who created this masterpiece but he died just ***before completion and missed the opening ceremony****.*

31st October

Born today in 1828 England was Joseph Swan and it was he who invented the Electric light bulb receiving patent No: 4933. His light bulbs lit up the world's first all electric building the Savoy Theatre and his home town ***football ground is now called the Stadium of Light****.*

31st October

The forgotten astronaut of Apollo 11 was born today in 1930 and his name was Michael Collins. Plaudits for the first moon landing always go to Armstrong and Aldrin with barely a mention for the third man who went ***all that way and never put a foot on the moon.***

November

This is the Month that takes it's Name from the Latin 'novem' meaning Nine as it was once the Ninth Month of the Year.

November has a Greek God named Scorpio who was said to be So Handsome that Apollo was Riddled with Envy

The 30 Days that make up November Start with the Day of the Dead and Finish With the Feast of St. Andrew

This Month is Gloriously Sunny and Warm in the Southern Hemisphere but up in the North the Cold takes Hold

The Birthstone of November is Topaz symbolising Friendship and the Two Signs of the Zodiac are Scorpio and Sagittarius

The Full Moon of November is Named After The Busy Beavers Building their Dams so is called the Beaver Moon

Thanksgiving in America Takes Place Each Year on the Third Thursday in November and is Followed by Black Friday

Playwright William Shakespeare wrote 154 Sonnets and 37 Plays but Did Not Ever Mention the Month of November

That's a Fact !!

1st November

*Cool Hand Luke released today in 1967 starred Paul Newman as the chain-gang prisoner who refuses to follow the rules and this is a true must-see movie with many iconic scenes. A car wash, 50 boiled eggs and the line "**what we've got here is failure to communicate**".*

1st November

*The home to the President opened today in 1800 Washington DC with John Adams it's first occupant. The building wasn't white and was generally referred to as President's House and although no President has ever been born **in the White House 2 of them have died there.***

2nd November

*The future King Edward V was born this day in 1470 and became King just 13 years later. Edward's life was thwart with danger and within a year of his ascension he and his brother were put into the Tower of London by their nice **Uncle Richard and were never seen again.***

2nd November

*The opening ceremony of Britain's M1 motorway took place today in 1959 and with it opened Watford Gap. This motorway stretches from London to Leeds and though it's 193 miles long it's not Britain's longest motorway **and the Watford Gap is nowhere near Watford.***

3rd November

Thirteen years on from 9/11 the One World Trade Center opened today in Downtown Manhattan NYC . Replacing the Twin Towers this 109 story skyscraper was built to an architectural height of 1,776 feet commemorating the year 1776 when America declare independence.

3rd November

The Russians sent Sputnik II into space today in 1957 and the stray dog named Laika who was onboard became the first animal to orbit the Earth. The flight paved the way for humans in space but it proved fatal for Laika who ***would probably have just settled for a nice bone.***

4th November

The Tomb of Egyptian King Tutankhamen was discovered today in 1922 by archaeologist Howard Carter in the Valley of the Kings. It's not really known if there was a curse put on the King's Tomb or not but what is known ***is that Tutankhamen died of a broken leg.***

4th November

Nazi General Field Marshall Rommel was getting destroyed by the Allies today in 1942 at the 2nd battle El Alamein so he completely disobeyed Adolf Hitler's orders and began the retreat of his forces. Maybe he thought ***to himself - blow this for a game of soldiers.***

5th November

Remember, remember the fifth of November Gunpowder Treason and Plot I see no reason why Gunpowder Treason should ever be forgot. Written to remember the failed attempt tonight in 1605 to blow up Protestant ***King James I and the Houses of Parliament.***

5th November

Robert Catesby planned the gunpowder plot and it was Guy Fawkes who was caught red handed this night in 1605 attempting to carry out the deadly deed. Fawkes gave his name as Johnny Johnson but after being brutally ***tortured by the King he admitted his guilt****.*

5th November

The year was 1688 when William of Orange arrived on English soil this November day. William had been invited by Protestant noblemen known as the 'Immortal Seven' to oust Catholic King James II and this was the start of what ***became known as the Glorious Revolution.***

6th November

Abraham Lincoln won the vote today in 1660 to become the country's 16th President. Lincoln's 6'4" figure had loomed large over his rivals and he became the country's first Republican President but sadly he would become the ***first of four Presidents to be assassinated.***

6th November

Abraham Lincoln was voted in as 16th American President today in 1860 making him the first Republican to hold the highest office in the the land. When Lincoln made his second inauguration speech his soon to be assassin was ***standing right there in the crowd watching him.***

6th November

Born today in Belgium 1814 was Antoine-Joseph Sax and throughout his childhood was condemned to misfortune. He fell from 3 stories high, hit his head on a rock, swallowed a pin, almost drowned and survived poisoning but ***what he did best was invent the Saxophone****.*

7th November

Butch Cassidy and the Sundance kid were outnumbered, cornered and killed in a bloody shootout in Bolivia this November day in 1908. The two notorious train and bank robbers were later immortalised in film with ***Paul Newman and Robert Redford as Butch & Sundance.***

7th November

Tyburn was a small village stood near what is now Marble Arch and for a long time was the place of public execution for criminals and traitors. But this Winnter's day in 1783 the last public execution took place when a guy named ***John Austen was the last man left hanging****.*

7th November

Franklyn Delano Roosevelt was well liked by the American public for he was voted in as President today in 1944 for a record fourth term. This would be the last time at the top for the President who suffered from polio as ***his life would end before his term would finish****.*

8th November

Robert Catesby was cornered and killed this November day in 1605 three days after Guy Fawkes was caught red-handed and the Gun-Powder plot uncovered. The Catholic Catesby was the mind behind the plan to blow up Parliament and Kill the Protestant King.

8th November

English astronomer Edmund Halley was born today in 1656 and he correctly predicted the arrival of the Comet now named after him. Seeing the comet just once in his lifetime his predictions of future arrivals have all come true ***and his Comet is next due in July 2061.***

8th November

Born this day in 1927 Knotty Ash was a true comic genius the late great Sir Ken Dodd who introduced the world to the Diddy men, the Jam Butty mines and his Tickling stick. Doddy is even the subject of a tough tongue twister ***which goes - Ken Dodd's Dad's Dog's Dead.***

9th November

It was this early November evening the Great Boston Fire of 1872 got started and blazed away for a full 12 hours before fire fighters got it under control. People were in shock as 13 lives were lost and the fire still ranks as ***one of the costliest disasters in American history****.*

9th November

Following years of speculation and debate the Death Penalty was abolished in Great Britain today in 1965 just one year after the last executions had taken place. Over the years people had been hanged for many different crimes ***ranging from murder to stealing cheese.***

9th November

When Rolling Stone magazine was published for the first time this November day in 1967 there was a host of names who's face could feature on the launch cover. They deliberated but knew there could be only one - ***his surname was Lennon and first name was John****.*

10th November

A sensational victory for publishers Penguin Books in the Old Bailey today in 1960 meant they could legally publish a sexually explicit and highly obscene novel. Following the ruling there was a stampede as people rushed to buy ***the rude book entitled Lady Chatterley's Lover.***

10th November

Gangster movie 'Angels with filthy Souls' premiered tonight in 1990 but audiences were watching a fictitious movie within-a-movie. Gun-toting gangster Johnny unleashed a blaze of machine-gun fire then famously yelled ***"Keep the change, ya Filthy Animal".***

10th November

*The United States US Marine Corps were founded today in 1775 just a month after the US Navy. Both were launched in preparation for the soon to be War of Independence against Britain andyears later led to the famous phrase by John Wayne "**So you wanna be a Marine**".*

10th November

Missing British explorer and missionary David Livingstone was found safe and well today in 1871 by Henry Morton Stanley whilst he was searching through the African bush. Upon spotting the explorer it is said the delighted ***Stanley exclaimed "Dr Livingstone I presume".***

11th November - Wear Your Poppy with Pride

Armistice Day today and it is well documented with good reason that the City of Liverpool was a base for wartime operations during WWI. People took to the challenge with bravery, tactical intelligence, and defiance, ultimately ***playing a crucial role in the nation's victory.***

11th November

Warren Harding was the 29th President of America and his time in office wasn't exactly a success. But it was he who dedicated America's tomb of the unknown soldier at Arlington cemetery today in 1921 ***on the third anniversary of armistice day.***

11th November

Leonardo De Caprio was born this November day in 1974 and was catapulted to superstardom 24 years later when he played Jack Dawson in Titanic. Most of his lines in the movie were scripted but one that wasn't ***was when Jack shouts "I'm the King of the world"****.*

11th November

A ceremony took place in Westminster Abbey today exactly two years after Armistice day as the Tomb of the Unknown Warrior was buried. A corresponding ceremony took place at the Arc de Triomphe and these two graves were ***first to honour the unknown dead in WWI.***

12th November

A tent discovered today in 1912 on the Ross Ice Shelf in Antarctica meant an 8 month search had reached it's conclusion. Inside the tent lay the frozen bodies of explorers Scott, Bowers and Wilson but the only thing removed ***from this Icy tomb was Scott's diary of events.***

12th November

King Canute was the King of England who sat at the edge of the sand trying, without success, to command the tide. Doing so, not for vanity but to prove to his subjects that he was a King and not a God. Canute the Great ***reigned until his death, this day in 1035 AD.***

12th November

A novel published today in 1880 was written by a soldier named Lew Wallace and the name he gave his story was "Ben Hur: A Tale of The Christ". The story became an Oscar winning epic and the novel turned its author into ***a very happy 'Soldier of Fortune'.***

12th November

Following the passing of King Canute it was Harold I who ascended to the English throne this November day in 1035 even though he wasn't the rightful heir. The new King had stolen the throne from his half-brother and his reign ***lasted exactly 4 years, 4 months and 4 days.***

13th November

A new new type of restaurant opened in the UK this very morning in 1974 and it was a bit different than usual as there were no plates and no cutlery. They sold burgers with fries all wrapped in paper and the staff said "have a nice day" - ***McDonald's had arrived in Britain****.*

13th November

A boy born today in London's East End in 1927 became the notorious gangland criminal George Cornell of the Richardson gang. He was fearless they said but he would end up dead when shot in the head by gangster Ronnie Kray ***in a pub called The Blind Beggar.***

13th November

Born today in 1312 was English warrior king Edward III who took no prisoners, executing his father's murderer, banishing his mother and declaring war on France which would last over 100 years. Edward III also created the ***Order of the Garter under the banner of St George****.*

13th November

Gioachino Rossini was nicknamed the 'Italian Mozart' he wrote Thieving Magpie, the William Tell Overture and plenty more. Rossini lived a superstitious life and always spent Friday 13th alone and he was alone when ***he died suddenly in 1658 on Friday 13th November.***

14th November

The first ever official UK No1 single 'Here in my Heart' sung by Al Martino hit the top spot this day in 1952 and stayed there for nine weeks making it the first ever UK Christmas No1. Then twenty years later ***Al Martino starred as Johnny Fontane in The Godfather.***

14th November

The life of England's most famous Royal mistress came to an end today in 1687 and she was the well known and well liked, Nell Gwyn. Charles II was her King but Nell called him her 'Charles the first' and of all the mistresses this ***King had known, none were quite like Nell****.*

14th November

Princess Anne married Captain Mark Phillips today in 1973 and although it was dubbed the Wedding of the Year the marriage would ultimately fail. Anne's big day had arrived on the same day as the 25th birthday of her brother ***and heir to the throne Prince Charles.***

15th November

The famous 'March to the Sea' by General William Sherman and his troops got under way this day in 1864 during the American civil war. As Sherman marched through Georgia his aim was to destroy everything in his path ***and crush the resolve of the confederates.***

15th November

A big moment on UK Television today in 1969 saw the first advert ever shown in COLOUR and it was for Birds Eye Garden Peas which aired during an episode of Thunderbirds. But most people watched it in black & white as ***few families actually owned of a colour TV set.***

15th November

*There have been some outstanding football captains and one of them, Ron Yeats who was born today in 1937 and captained Liverpool during the heyday of the 1960's. Bill Shankly called him 'Colossus' and **told the press to "go take a walk around him"**.*

16th November

*King Edward I ascended to the English throne following the death of his father this winters day in 1272. Known as 'Hammer of the Scots' Edward was a ruthless King and anyone found guilty of his newly introduced crime of **High Treason were hanged, drawn & quartered.***

16th November

*There was a whole lotta shakin' going on tonight in 1957 thanks to the 2i's Coffee Bar in London which was being used by the BBC to broadcast their all new 'Six-Five Special' music show. On that night this tiny little coffee bar became **the birthplace of British Rock-n-Roll.***

16th November

*When David Livingstone gazed upon a giant waterfall in Zimbabwe this November day in 1855 he couldn't believe his eyes. He named it Victoria Falls after his beloved Queen but the locals were far more creative because **they called it 'The Smoke That Thunders'.***

17th November

The Year was 1603 and Sir Walter Raleigh found himself under arrest today on charges of Treason after annoying King James I once too often. Raleigh was fortunate to avoid the block on this occasion but it was only a matter of time ***before his head would finally roll.***

17th November

Elizabeth I became the last Tudor monarch when she succeeded her half-sister Mary today in 1558. During the Elizabeth's 'Golden age' treachery was always abound but the Queen kept her enemies at bay and in 1588 she ***even fought off the might of the Spanish Armada.***

17th November

When the life of England's most hated Queen came to an end this afternoon in 1558 most people shed not a tear. This was Bloody Mary the Catholic who not only beheaded Lady Jane Grey but loathed Protestants so much she ***had hundreds of them burned to death.***

18th November

WWI was raging in 1916 when British General Haig finally called an end to the bloody Battle of the Somme today. For more than four months soldiers had leapt from their trenches to fight the enemy through many miles of mud and ***casualties were more than a million***

18th November

Swiss folk hero William Tell stood straight, took aim and fired the bolt from his crossbow right through the apple that sat upon his young son's head in 1307 this November day. The great Tell then killed the man who ***forced him to do the deed that he didn't want to do****.*

18th November

This was the day in 1928 Walt Disney launched his first short film to have synchronised sound and with it a colourful new character was born named Mickey Mouse. Business got bigger and better for Walt but he never forgot it ***all started with a mouse in Steamboat Willie****.*

19th November

Born this day in the year 1600 was England's future King Charles I and he was the King whose Royalist Cavaliers fought the English civil war against Oliver Cromwell's Roundheads. Charles remains the only King to be found ***guilty of treason and have his head chopped off.***

19th November

People listened as the President spoke "Four score and seven years ago our fathers brought forth on this continent a new nation, conceived in liberty and dedicated to the proposition that all men are created equal" Lincoln's ***Gettysburg Address delivered today in 1863***

19th November

When the first National Lottery was drawn this evening in 1994 most people won nothing but 5 lucky ticket holders did share the jackpot. Today the lottery costs twice as much to enter and the chances of winning even less ***than back then - but you just never know.***

20th November

The Year was 1945 and 24 prominent leaders of Nazi German's Third Reich were finally brought to face trial today for war crimes.The trials were held in Nuremberg by Allied forces under international law and were described as ***the "greatest trials in history" by a British judge.***

20th November

Comedian Bob Hope was guest of honour at the Miss World Beauty pageant today in 1970 when he was pelted with bags of flour thrown from the audience by demonstrators. But the good news for everyone watching was ***the flour pelting was much funnier than his jokes.***

20th November

Since 1789 the USA have appointed 46 Presidents and there has been a whole host different personalities amongst them. There are the good the bad the terrible and even the just plain stupid but their latest appointment ***was born today in 1942 and he is Joe Biden.***

21st November

The Year was 1980 and for MGM Grand Hotel in Nevada it was business as usual today as the place was packed out. Then without warning a deadly fire broke out resulting in the deaths of 87 people and further 650 injured ***in the worst disaster in Nevada history.***

21st November

Frankenstein the movie premiered on the big screen this cold November night in 1931 and movie-goers went along for a fright night. Mary Shelley's chilling novel had been brought to life and it was Boris Karloff ***who played the monster with nuts in his neck.***

21st November

A movie hit the big screen this evening in New York City 1976 which made Sylvester Stallone a Hollywood superstar overnight. This was the rags to riches story of Rocky the local boy who made good and of all the movies released ***that year - this one really packed a punch.***

21st November

The Pilgrim Fathers reached America today aboard their famous ship 'Mayflower' in 1620 having left England two months earlier. But the Pilgrims had an almighty shock as they were hit with a treacherous winter and ***only half their number survived to see the Spring.***

22nd November

This Friday afternoon 1963 in downtown Dallas John F Kennedy was assassinated and became the 4th President to die by the bullet. JFK is the only one shot with a rifle, the only catholic, the only Democrat and much ***controversy surrounds his assassination to this day.***

22nd November

Toy Story introduced the world to Woody, Buzz Lightyear and a host of other toys on the big screen this very day in 1992 and it became such a soaraway success that sequels would soon follow. Much has been said about these toys ***that have gone "To infinity and beyond".***

22nd November

When Lyndon Baines Johnson was sworn in as 36th American President today in 1963 he was aboard Airforce One. Standing with him was Jacqueline Kennedy, her pale pink outfit covered in the blood of her husband JFK who ***had been assassinated just hours earlier****.*

22nd November

England won the Rugby World Cup today in 2003 beating Australia thanks to a drop-kick by Johnny Wilkinson seconds before the end of extra time. Watched by millions across the globe England became the first ***Northern Hemisphere team to win the Webb Ellis Trophy.***

23rd November

Three men known as the Manchester Martyrs were hanged today in 1867 at Salford Gaol in front of a crowd of almost 10,000 people. The three had been found guilty of murdering a police sergeant and setting free two convicts ***during the violent hold-up of a police van.***

23rd November

*The World's first Juke Box was introduced in San Francisco today in 1889 and all you had to do was put your coin in, pick your tune and play it loud. This invention soon went global and people would one day hear the Rubettes singing '****Come on baby do the Jukebox Jive****'.*

23rd November

The humble Pencil Sharpener was patented today in 1897 by J L Love and many a pencil has been sharpened on one ever since. I'm not exactly sure where Love got the idea from for his pencil sharpener but it could have been ***when he watched a cat running away from him.***

23rd November

It was today in 1963 children and a few adults across the UK dived behind their sofa and dared to peep at the TV as a new series started on BBC in black and white. One of the scariest introductions to any programme ever ***the unforgettable soundtrack of Dr Who.***

24th November

One of the world's best selling books was published today in 1877 a 255 page novel by Anna Sewell telling the heartwarming story of Black Beauty. Her beautiful horse is famous in film and TV but sadly Anna died ***before she could enjoy the success of her masterpiece.***

24th November

When news broke announcing the death of Freddie Mercury this very evening in 1991 Freddy's fans and the music world were in mourning. The charismatic frontman had turned Queen into a global supergroup and although others have tried, ***no-one has the magic of Mercury.***

24th November

Two days after the assassination of JFK in 1963 prime suspect Lee Harvey Oswald was in police custody when he was shot and killed by a night club owner named Jack Ruby. The shooting of Oswald was broadcast live on TV ***and Ruby was labelled the assassin's assassin****.*

24th November

A must-see cult classic hit the big screen today in 1966 and admirers were aplenty. This was One Million Years BC starring sex-symbol Raquel Welch and the movie's defining image of Raquel became the final poster ***on Andy's prison wall in The Shawshank Redemption.***

25th November

A baby born today in 1960 was named after his famous father who had just been voted 35th President of America. On the same day in 1963 this boy should have been enjoying his third birthday party but instead ***he was standing with his mother at his father's funeral.***

25th November

Today in 1994 in Notting Hill 36 pop stars recorded "Do they know it's Christmas?" The song became the festive favourite that year and again with different line-ups 1989 & 2004. Raising money to fight famine in Ethiopia it ***was written by two men named Bob & Midge.***

25th November

Two men who had been murdered within two days of each other were both buried this November day in 1963 after been pronounced dead in the same hospital. One of them was President John Fitzgerald Kennedy and the other ***was the alleged assassin Lee Harvey Oswald.***

25th November

Today in 1953 the English international football team suffered their worst ever defeat on home soil. Hungary destroyed England 6-3 at Wembley in a match dubbed 'Game of the Century' Six months later England went to Hungary ***for a replay and received a 7-1 thrashing.***

26th November

The iconic supersonic passenger aircraft Concorde took to the skies this sunny day in 2003 for its final ever flight. Flying London to Bristol meant a short trip to retirement for this magnificent majestic bird of paradise after which - ***The Concorde roar would be heard no more****.*

26th November

Born this winter's day in 1939 within the city limits of Nutbush USA was Tina Turner and her life story has been well documented in book and film. This multi-talented superstar has a string of hits both sides of the Atlantic and ***arguably her most famous is (simply) "The Best"****.*

26th November

Notorious Punk Rock group the Sex Pistols shocked the establishment again today in 1976 when they released their single 'Anarchy in the UK'. Johnny Rotten and Sid Vicious had burst onto the music scene without a care and they ***were loved by Punk Rockers everywhere****.*

27th November

Little Big Horn made him famous but today in 1868 General Custer and his 7th Cavalry needlessly attacked the Cheyenne camp of Chief Black Kettle. Women children and braves were slaughtered in this unprovoked attack ***which is known as the Washita Massacre.***

27th November

One of the world's most influential martial arts experts ever to grace the Earth was born this November day in San Francisco 1940. An icon of the 20th century and star of must see movies such as Fist of Fury and Enter the Dragon ***- The one and only multi-talented Bruce Lee****.*

28th November

When 'She Loves You' hit the top of charts today in 1963 it was the second time the song had reached No1. 'She Loves You' also became the best selling single of the decade and the first for the Fab Four to sell over a million ***copies****...............* ***And you know that can't be bad.***

28th November

Wedding Bells were ringing in Stratford-upon-Avon this winter's day in 1582 as William Shakespeare married Anne Hathaway. The two caused a bit of a scandal at the time as Anne was eight years older than her husband and ***several months pregnant with their first child****.*

28th November

One of the most infamous Pirates ever to sail the seven seas was Captain Blackbeard and today in 1717 he attacked and captured French ship 'La Concorde'. He then renamed her 'Queen Anne's Revenge' ***after his beloved Queen, whether she liked it or not.***

29th November

When the life of Hollywood heart-throb Cary Grant ended quietly today in 1986 he was 82 years old. The leading male in many a movie, this was the man with the unique transatlantic accent who was British born in Bristol ***and his birth name was Archibald Leach.***

29th November

Oh yeah I'll tell you something, I think you'll understand, When I'll say that something, I want to hold your hand, I want to hold your hand.... Released today in 1963 this little beauty became Christmas No:1 for the Fab-Four and over the next few years ***there would be three more****.*

29th November

The life of the talented British racing driver Graham Hill ended in tragedy today in 1975 when the aircraft he was piloting crashed during thick fog. Graham had won two Formula 1 championships and is the only man ever ***to win motor racing's illustrious 'Triple Crown'.***

30th November

The first ever football international match took place this November day in 1872 when Scotland hosted England and the score was 0-0. Since then England have won most encounters but when England were world champions ***the first team to beat them was Scotland.***

30th November

*Scotland and other countries celebrate the feast day of St. Andrew the apostle this November day each year. When Andrew faced crucifixion today in 60AD he asked to be tied to an X shaped cross as he felt **unworthy of dying on the Same shaped cross as Jesus**.*

30th November

*Danish King Canute ascended to the English throne today in 1016 following the passing of Edmund II and his reign lasted almost 19 yrs. Canute is the wise old King who proved to his people he wasn't a God by making them watch as **he famously tried to command the tide.***

December

The Last Month of the Year is Here and is Named after the Latin 'decem' as way Back Then It was Month Number Ten

The Greek God of December is Zeus - Almighty God of Sky and Thunder who Rules as King of the Gods of Mount Olympus

Christmas has been Celebrated in December since 337 AD Following an Announcement by the Pope a Year Earlier

There is a Saying that goes "If Snow Falls on Christmas Day then Easter will be Warm, Green and Sunny".

The Birthstone for the Month of December is Turquoise and the Two Zodiac Signs are Sagittarius and Capricorn

The Winter Solstice arrives this Month in the Northern Hemisphere and the Full Moon of December is the Cold Moon

It was Late December King Herod is said to have Ordered All Baby Boys be Put to Death in an Attempt to Kill Baby Jesus

December is a Very Superstitious Month So it's Always Wise to Make Sure you are Careful What you Wish For

That's a Fact !!

1st December

The world's most famous fictional detective first appeared in print this December day in 1887 as Arthur Conan Doyle's novel 'A Study in Scarlett' was finally published. Avid readers everywhere soon got to know the violin-playing ***Sherlock Holmes of 221b Baker Street****.*

1st December

After Simon de Montford formed the first English parliament in 1265 men occupied every seat until this day 1919 when Lady Nancy Astor became the first woman to take her place in the House of Commons but Lady ***Nancy Astor wasn't British, she was actually American****.*

2nd December

Nick Leeson was General Manager for Barings Finance but today in 1995 he was in court charged with fraud. Guilty was the verdict and he was sentenced to 6.5 years in prison but it didn't help Barings as they went bust and ***Leeson is the man who literally 'Broke the Bank'.***

2nd December

Napoleon Bonaparte had declared himself Emperor of France, a fitting title for the greatest leader the French had ever known and it was this Sunday in 1804 with Josephine at his side, Napoleon's coronation took place ***at Notre Dame, making his new title official.***

3rd December

Nobody knew at the time but when the Beatles went on stage in Glasgow this evening in 1965 it was the beginning of their final UK Tour in the UK and it finished nine days later in Cardiff. Pretty soon the Fab Four would ***board a plane and roar away to the USA.***

3rd December

Millions of text messages are sent every day across the world but the very first text message was sent this December day in 1992 when Engineer Neil Papworth messaged his friend Andrew Jarvis across the Vodafone network with ***two popular words 'Merry Christmas'.***

4th December

The world's most expensive box of eggs sold today in a 2006 Los Angeles auction where an anonymous buyer forked out $420,000 for 22 dinosaur eggs with embryos. The 65 million year old eggs were all broken but ***it wasn't because they'd just been under the hammer.***

4th December

Of all the men chosen to serve as Pope only one Englishman has ever worn the Fishermans Ring and he was appointed this day in 1154. Nicholas Brakespear was known as Pope Adrian IV but his reign was shorter than most as ***after five years he went to meet his maker.***

4th December

Born this day in 1940 was a boy named Gary Gilmore who became a convicted murderer at the age of 37 and famously demanded to be given the death penalty. The Judge duly obliged and after his death a Punk Rock group ***sang - Looking through Gary Gilmore's eyes.***

5th December

At the age of just 35 the life of composer Wolfgang Amadeus Mozart came to an end In the early hours of this bleak December morning in 1791. Just a handful of mourners attended his funeral but the cause of death of this music ***Maestro remains one of history's mysteries.***

5th December

A boy born today in the USA in 1839 became one of the country's most ferocious military men who cut his teeth in the American civil war. He was George Armstrong Custer but along with his infamous 7th Cavalry ***Custer ended up being slaughtered at Little Big Horn****.*

5th December

Discovered adrift and deserted on the Atlantic Ocean this day in 1872 was 'Ghost Ship' the Mary Celeste, her cargo was all intact but her captain, passengers and crew, were nowhere to be seen and to this very day ***their disappearance remains a mystery in history.***

6th December

The building of the world's most famous obelisk was finally complete today in 1884. The iconic marble structure which towers over 500ft high into the American sky is named after their first President and is recognisable ***across the globe as the Washington Monument.***

6th December

England's future King Henry VI was born today in 1421, he would never meet his father and at nine months of age became King. Henry was murdered in the Tower of London during the Wars of the Roses and remains ***the only man crowned King of England and France.***

6th December

The ratification of the 21st Amendment today in 1933 had People celebrating into the night as Prohibition in America ended after thirteen years. This Amendment is the only one ever to overturn another and ***it had the full support President F.D Roosevelt.***

7th November

It was lift-off for NASA's last ever manned mission to the Moon today in 1972 when Apollo 17 left Cape Canaveral and thundered into Space. There were 7 manned missions to the Moon and 6 of them were successful ***but the one that wasn't was Apollo 13.***

7th December

Trekkies everywhere enjoyed a universal treat today in 1979 as Star Trek the movie premiered 10 years after the TV series ended. Once again James Tiberius Kirk, Mr Spock and the crew could boldly go where no man had gone before, ***Star Trekking Across the Universe.***

7th December

It was this morning in 1941 Japanese planes attacked Pearl Harbour destroying the American base in Hawaii and over 2,400 people were killed. President Roosevelt's response was swift and true as he declared war on Japan the ***following day and America entered WWII***

8th December

Born today 1542 a baby girl who six days later became Mary Queen of Scots, some years later Mary was forced to abdicate and flee to England but Elizabeth I saw her as a threat and kept her locked up, then at the age of 44 ***Mary was beheaded in Fotheringhay castle.***

8th December

The world was in shock this evening in 1980 following the news that former Beatle and charismatic frontman John Lennon had been shot and killed right outside his New York apartment. A cruel and shocking end to the life of ***the man who just wanted to give peace a chance.***

9th December

Smog and smoke that had smothered London over 4 days finally lifted this December evening in 1952 but not before 4,000 people in the city had lost their lives. The Capital was a different place back then and still today, ***London is referred to by many as 'The Smoke'.***

9th December

The cobbles of Coronation Street made their first TV appearance this Winter evening in 1960 and the first words spoken were "Now the next thing you'll want to do is get a sign-writer in". Corrie is not doing too bad ***for a show was only meant to have 13 episodes.***

9th December

Half a league, half a league, half a league onward into the valley of death rode the six hundred.... Alfred Lord Tennyson's famous poem published this day 1854 in memory of those who gave their lives at the ill-fated ***Charge of the Light Brigade during the Crimean war.***

10th December

Traffic lights have been around for twenty years 'Longer' than cars and the first set were installed this December day in 1868 outside Westminster Palace. Thousands of sets have since been installed and the traffic in ***London moves no faster now than it did then.***

10th December

King Edward VIII signed his Instrument of Abdication this December day in 1936 making it a year with Three Kings. Edward stepped away from the throne to marry American divorcee Mrs Simpson and some time later ***his wife said to him - You can't abdicate and eat it.***

10th December

A long awaited movie premiered on the big screen tonight in 1978 and cinemas were packed to the rafters with excited moviegoers. Superman was in town with Christopher Reeve brilliantly playing the flying Man of Steel ***and his fumbling alter-ego Clark Kent.***

10th December

After reading a news article condemning him for profiteering Sir Alfred Nobel bequeathed his entire fortune to the Nobel Prize today in 1896 just before he died. Alfred held hundreds of different patents during his lifetime ***but his most famous was just Dynamite.***

11th December

As James II tried to flee England this December day in 1688 following the Glorious Revolution he threw the Great Seal of the Realm into the River Thames. James was caught by men loyal to William of Orange and the ***Great Seal of the Realm was caught by a fisherman.***

11th December

With the Revolution in full throttle and his country in turmoil things got even worse for Louis XVI today in 1792 when he found himself on trial facing charges of treason. The French King knew deep down that sooner or later ***he would be under the cold Blade of Death.***

11th December

This was the day in 1936 George VI ascended to the British throne as the third monarch from the House of Windsor. His coronation took place within five months of his ascension, he used the day that had been set for ***his brother Edward VIII who had just abdicated.***

11th December

Muhammad Ali stepped into the boxing ring tonight in 1981 to take on Trevor Berbick. This 10 round 'Drama in Bahama' ended with a unanimous points victory for Berbick and for the man who called himself the greatest it ***was the last night he would ever fight.***

12th December

The Beatles performed their last official UK concert this December evening in 1965 to a sell out crowd of 5,000 ecstatic fans inside Cardiff's Capitol Theatre. There was never another UK tour from the Fab Four and ***as for Cardiff's Capitol Theatre it is no more.***

12th December

The multi-award winning musical Saturday Night Fever premiered this December evening in 1977 and the world went disco crazy. The dancing and the music were so good that young men everywhere wanted ***dance moves like John Travolta and Teeth like the Bee Gees.***

12th December

The year was 1800 and America needed a capital city so today they chose Washington D.C. which seemed like a good idea at the time because the White House had just been built there. Washington D.C. is not one of the 50 States ***but there is a State called Washington****.*

12th December

Old Blue Eyes himself Frank Sinatra was born today in 1915 he became a screen legend and one of the best selling music artists of all time. Frank is now long gone but inside his coffin are his remains, a bottle of ***Jack Daniels and a packet of Camel cigarettes****.*

13th December

It was this day in 1577 Francis Drake set sail from England with the blessing of the Queen to circumnavigate the globe and he returned three years later aboard the Golden Hind then soon after was knighted ***aboard this very ship by his Queen Elizabeth I.***

13th December

Movie star James Dean started his acting career this December day in 1950 when he starred in a TV commercial for the lip smacking thirst quenching drink Pepsi Cola. Although Dean's career was cut tragically short it didn't stop him ***becoming a twentieth century cultural icon.***

13th December

Unlucky 13 struck for Saddam Hussein today in 2003 as Operation Red Dawn concluded with the capture of this Iraqi dictator. Hussein was wanted for crimes against humanity when American soldiers dragged him ***from his favourite hiding place - A Hole in the ground.***

13th December

This Winter's day in 1961 saw the end of the life of much loved American folk artist Grandma Moses. This incredibly talented lady who picked up the paintbrush well after her 70th birthday could paint both left and right handed ***had lived to the grand age of 101.***

14th December

American Astronaut Eugene Cernan became the last man to step off the Moon when he did so today in 1972. Mankind has never yet returned to the Moon but its surface has been left littered with over 50 tons of discarded ***machinery left behind by six Apollo missions.***

14th December

When the future King George VI was born today in 1895 it was a bitter-sweet moment for his Queen Victoria. Whilst the Queen was happy to greet her grandson she couldn't forget this was also the 24th anniversary of ***the death of her beloved husband Prince Albert****.*

14th December

On this very day in 1911 Swedish explorer Ronald Amundsen and his team of five became the first people ever to brave the Antarctic and make it to the South Pole. Not only did the men survive the sub-zero temperatures ***they also lived long enough to tell the tale.***

14th December

Liverpool football club are one of the most decorated clubs in world football with a host of trophies that many a club would be proud to boast and the rise to greatness started this December day in 1959 with the ***appointment of the charismatic Bill Shankly.***

15th December

The famous phrase 'Elvis has left the building' was first used this December evening in 1956 when a night club manager had to stop the crowd from shouting for Elvis to return to the stage as another act was waiting to perform ***and Elvis really had left the building.***

15th December

*A movie released today in 1939 became the must see Hollywood Blockbuster Gone With the Wind which told the tale of Scarlett O'Hara and Rhett Butler. Scarlett said "**After all tomorrow is another day**" and Rhett said **"Frankly my dear I don't give a damn"**.*

15th December

*Nazi war criminal Adolf Eichmann was sentenced to Death today in 1961 after being found Guilty of war crimes at his trial in Jerusalem. Eichmann who had evaded capture for 15 years showed no remorse and was **described by the Judge as 'The Banality of Evil'.***

16th December

*At 10 years and 10 days old England's King Henry VI was crowned King of France today in 1431 much to the annoyance of the French. Notre Dam Cathedral hosted the ceremony as Henry VI became King of both countries and it was **all thanks to his dad King Henry V.***

16th December

*Jane Austen born this December day in Hampshire 1775 became one of the world's greatest ever novelists. During her relatively short life Jane penned some of the best novels ever written and all Janeites know her famous **'six of the best' that stand out from the rest.***

16th December

The English civil war was over, the monarchy had fallen and today in 1653 'old ironsides' Oliver Cromwell was appointed Lord Protector of the commonwealth of England, Scotland and Ireland. But Cromwell's military rule was ***ruthless and cruel and he even banned Christmas.***

16th December

On this sunny afternoon in 1773 Americans, disguised as British sailers in Boston harbour boarded a British ship and threw all it's cargo overboard into the water in protest of taxes imposed by King George III. ***The event is widely known as The Boston Tea Party.***

17th December

When the Wright brothers completed the first heavier than air manned flight today in 1903 it was Orville at the controls. The flight of the 'Flyer' lasted 59.4 seconds and the distance flown was actually shorter than ***the wingspan of today's largest aeroplane.***

17th December

When notorious King Henry VIII fell out again today with the Pope in 1538 he cared not a jot. The King had the son he always wanted, had put himself in charge of a new Church of England and was keeping busy searching for ***a woman daft enough to be his fourth wife.***

17th December

The seventeenth Prime Minister of Australia went for a dip in the ocean this sunny down under day in 1967 and disappeared beneath the waves never to be seen again. His name was Harold Holt and forty years later ***an official enquiry decided he must have drowned.***

18th December

Born this day in London 1778 was Joseph Grimaldi and he became known as the Clown with 'The face that launched a thousand quips'. Although a Clown called Coco came along later it is Grimaldi who is recognised as the ***world's greatest and most famous Clown.***

18th December

The premier of must see movie 'The Pink Panther' showcased this December evening in 1963 and starred the late Peter Sellers as the accident prone fumbling French detective. Although the Pink Panther was mysterious and elusive ***we all know he came from Durham.***

18th December

Woodrow Wilson was the 28th USA President but he was widowed and wanted to remarry and this day 1915 he became the first sitting president to tie the knot when he married Edith Bolling. Whilst in office he suffered ill health ***so Edith would often run the country.***

18th December

Great train robber Ronnie Biggs bowed out today in 2013 at the age of 84 and he was without doubt the most famous of all the train robbers. Biggs managed to escape from prison, flee to France, then live in Australia and Brazil ***before returning home for his final years.***

19th December

When Emily Brontë died this day in 1848 aged just 30 her only novel Wuthering Heights had been in publication for just one year. Emily refused to see her doctor until it was too late but her famous novel lived on to be ***celebrated in film and also in song by Kate Bush.***

19th December

The original World Cup Trophy was stolen from Brazil's footballing headquarters today in 1983 and has never been found. This was the second theft of the famous trophy and although they had detectives on the case ***what they really needed was a dog named Pickles.***

19th December

Bill Clinton was impeached by the House of Representatives today in 1998 as pressure mounted over his relationship with a White House intern. The vultures circled and lawyers summoned but they couldn't trap the President - ***He was too smart, too quick and far too slick.***

19th December

The Plantagenets are the longest reigning dynasty in the history of our monarchy boasting fourteen kings who took to the throne and the very first of them had his coronation this winters day in 1194. He was King Henry II and his wife Eleanor of Acquatain was at his side.

20th December

England's Richard the Lionheart was trying to make his way back home via Austria this December evening in 1192 when he was kidnapped by his enemy Prince Leopold. Richard was held captive for fourteen months and England paid a 'kings ransom' to get him back.

20th December

A 35 year old man released from prison today in Germany 1924 had served just eight months of a five year prison sentence. If the authorities knew what they were unleashing on the world they may not have been so hasty ***to set free this prisoner named Adolf Hitler.***

20th December

In Germany 1812 the first collection of the Brother's Grimm Fairy Tales were published for all to see today. The 86 tales of wonder and intrigue which captivated people's imagination included Rapunzel, Sleeping Beauty, ***Snow White and the infamous.......Rumpelstiltskin.***

20th December

The famous Hoover Dam on the Colorado river stands over 700ft tall but it's construction cost the lives of almost 100 men. The last man fell to his death today in 1935 exactly thirteen years to the day after his father had ***fallen to his death also working on the Hoover Dam.***

21st December

This evening in 1988 Pan Am flight 103 left Heathrow on route to the USA but as the plane flew over Lockerbie an explosion ripped through the aircraft. This appalling act of terrorism was the result of a bomb in the luggage ***compartment and 270 people lost their lives.***

21st December

This December day 1929 circus performer Coco the Clown made his first Big-Top appearance. An excited audience watched eagerly as the colourful clown entered the arena and although some found Coco quite funny ***most of the children were absolutely terrified.***

21st December

Elvis Presley walked into the White House to meet Richard Nixon this December day in 1970 and received full VIP treatment even being presented with a narcotics badge that had his name on it. The King immediately returned the compliment ***and gave the President a Gun.***

21st December

Bashful, Doc, Dopey, Happy, Grumpy, Sleepy, Sneezy and of course, Snow White all hit the big screen today in 1937 as Snow White and the Seven Dwarfs became the first ever feature length cartoon to be released by the great man of imagination, Walt Disney.

22nd December

During the early days of British motorways people could travel as fast as they could get their car to go as there were no speed limits but that all ended this day in 1965 when the 70 mph maximum speed limit was introduced on motorways and rural roads across the uk.

22nd December

The iconic Brandenburg Gate separating East from West Germany was re-opened today in 1989 having been locked shut since the Berlin Wall was built. The wall itself had fallen over a month earlier so maybe todays opening was planned - ***Or maybe they'd lost the key.***

22nd December

British Prime Minister Winston Churchill arrived in Washington DC today in 1941 for a wartime conference with President Franklyn D. Roosevelt. America had joined WWII fourteen days earlier after declaring war on Japan ***following the attack on Pearl Harbour.***

22nd December

Boris Karloff had been making quite a name for himself as the main man for monster movies and tonight in 1932 he starred in another belter. This time Boris was wrapped in bandages from head to toe and gave a faultless ***performance as the original Mummy monster.***

23rd December

Filming of the famous movie The Wizard of Oz had to be halted today in 1938 as Margaret Hamilton's costume caught fire while she was wearing it. Health & Safety wasn't much of a priority back then and someone accidentally ***set fire - To The Wicked Witch of the West.***

23rd December

Blitzen, Comet, Cupid, Dasher, Dancer, Donner, Prancer and Vixen were introduced to the publishing world today in the 1823 poem 'The night before Christmas'. Then 116 years later Rudolph the Red Nosed Reindeer ***appeared in song and Rudolph is actually, a girl.***

23rd December

The brothers Grimm fairytale telling the tale of Hansel and Gretel premiered on stage this cold December evening in 1893 Germany and was hailed as 'Wunderbar'. The play was brilliantly written by the German composer who ***was known as Englebert Humperdinck.***

23rd December

'Twas the night before Christmas when all through the house, not a creature was stirring not even a mouse............. This famous piece of poetry was published today in 1823 and this meant the words were actually published, the night before, the night before Christmas.

24th December

Born Christmas Eve in 1166 was England's King John, it was he who granted the Royal Charter making Liverpool a borough and it was also King John who designed the original seven streets of Liverpool, one of which is Old Hall street on which the ECHO offices now stand.

24th December

In the the very early hours of this morning in 1888 tormented artist Vincent Van Gogh sliced off part of his left ear following an argument with house-mate and fellow artist Gauguin. It is believed Van Gogh then gave the severed ear ***to his favourite prostitute named Rachel.***

24th December

The iconic photograph showing planet Earth floating in the darkness of space known as 'Earthrise' was taken today in 1968 by Apollo VIII Astronauts. When the image was released to the watching world even the British ***Flat Earth Society accepted the Earth was Round.***

24th December

Born Christmas Eve 1945 was one of Rock music's most famous men, Ian Kilminster AKA 'Lemmy' the Godfather of Heavy Metal. This late great gravel voiced singer often said 'We are Motörhead and we play Rock n Roll so don't forget us' ***- Mötorhead fans certainly haven't.***

25th December

St.Paul's Cathedral was declared open today in 1711 even though the building wasn't quite complete. Christopher Wren had designed and built this magnificent structure on Ludgate Hill to deliberately stand at a height of ***365 feet at the highest point of the City of London.***

25th December

In 1932 George V was delivering the first Royal Christmas Day speech to a nation gathered around their radios listening to his words of wisdom when Crash Bang Wallop the King's chair collapsed. Maybe it was a wonky leg or ***maybe the King had eaten too much Turkey.***

25th December

The Year was 1914 and WWI had raged for almost five months when British and German soldiers along the Western Front laid down arms today to take an unofficial Christmas truce. Soldiers on both sides shook hands, ***swapped presents and even had a game of football.***

25th December

In the year 336 AD the Roman Church declared Christmas Day be celebrated on December 25th and ever since, we have celebrated the happy occasion with fun, festivities, turkey and stuffing, so in the words of a very famous song.......... 'Merry Christmas Everybody'.

26th December

It was 1973 and one of the most iconic films ever to hit the big screen premiered this evening to American audiences, many of whom were terrified by what they saw. Linda Blair starred as a young girl possessed by demons in ***this supernatural horror film - The EXORCIST***

26th December

American President Woodrow Wilson visited Britain this Boxing Day 1918 and became the first President ever to do so. Jubilant crowds lined the streets as the President accompanied King George V on route to Buckingham Palace ***through a sea of Red, White and Blue.***

26th December

The fall of the Soviet Union had been on the cards for some time when the inevitable happened today in 1991. In his memoirs years later Mikel Gorbachev wrote that the biggest contributor to the collapse was their ***handling of the nuclear disaster at Chernobyl.***

27th December

Benazir Bhutto was assassinated today in 2007 whilst inside a bomb proof vehicle. The former Prime Minister and first female to lead a Muslim nation had opened the vehicle's roof hatch to stand and wave to crowds when the ***deadly assassin struck with bullets and bomb.***

27th December

The world famous Radio City Music Hall in down town Manhattan NYC opened today in 1932 and its seating capacity of 5,960 made it the largest theatre in the world. Although the years may have taken their toll ***- this is still a great place to let the good times roll.***

27th December

When the life of 91 year old Gustave Eiffel ended today in 1923 he left the French with one of the most famous structures in the world. The Eiffel Tower should have lasted 20 years but thanks to Gustave's powers of persuasion ***this Parisian landmark still stands tall today.***

28th December

Eight days of brutal house to house fighting came to an end this December evening in 1943 when battle hardened Canadian Infantry defeated Germany's 1st Parachute Division. This crucial victory during WWII allowed the ***Canadians to take the Italian town of Ortona.***

28th December

When six year old Hollywood child superstar Shirley Temple sang "On the good ship Lollipop" today in 1934 it was during the launch of her latest movie 'Bright Eyes'. Many of those watching and listening didn't quite realise that ***the Good Ship Lollipop was an Aeroplane.***

28th December

Tragedy struck this Winter's evening in 1879 when the Tay Rail Bridge collapsed as a passenger train crossed over it during a violent storm. Everyone aboard the train perished in the waters below and subsequent ***investigations found the bridge design was to blame.***

29th December

This was not a good day to be a Chicken in Hong Kong in 1997 as the government started to slaughter every single one of the 1.25 million chickens in the country to stop the spread of deadly influenza. If you try you can ***say Hong Kong without moving your lips or tongue****.*

29th December

This day in 1890 American soldiers slaughtered almost 300 North American Indian men, women and children. Ghost Dancers led by Chief Big Foot had been surrounded attacked and murdered by U.S. Cavalry in the bloodbath ***known as 'Massacre of Wounded Knee'.***

30th December

The Battle of Wakefield which took place today in 1460 was one of the major conflicts of England's Wars of the Roses. Victory was decisive for the Lancastrians and of the 9,000 Yorkists who had marched into this bloody battle ***less than 7,000 marched out of it.***

30th December

Bobby Farrell of pop group Boney-M died unexpectedly tonight in 2010 St Petersburg. His group had once sang about Russian mystic Rasputin and the death of the Boney-M frontman coincided exactly with the death of ***Rasputin 94 years earlier also in St Petersburg.***

31st December

Scottish poet Robert Burns wrote lyrics to accompany a famous tune which gave the world 'Auld Land Syne' and this is the song so many will sing this very night. The words literally mean 'old long ago' and after singing this song ***the first word most people say is "Happy"****.*

31st December

The opening ceremony of the Millennium Wheel took place today in 1999 on the banks of the river Thames but there were no passengers on board. Now known as the London Eye this slow moving attraction towers 443ft and its ***32 pods represent the 32 London boroughs****.*

Lightning Source UK Ltd.
Milton Keynes UK
UKHW020642270421
382707UK00009B/212

9 781913 151492